Speak Up for Museums

Speak Up for Museums

The AAM Guide to Advocacy

By Gail Ravnitzky Silberglied
Director of Government Relations, AAM

Illustrations by Michael Balderrama

The AAM Press

AMERICAN ASSOCIATION OF MUSEUMS

1575 EYE STREET NW. SUITE 400
WASHINGTON DC 20005

WWW.AAM-US.ORG

Speak Up For Museums: The AAM Guide to Advocacy

By Gail Ravnitzky Silberglied

© 2011 The AAM Press, American Association of Museums, 1575 Eye St. NW, Suite 400, Washington, DC 20005

Silberglied, Gail Ravnitzky, 1969-
  Speak up for museums : the AAM guide to advocacy / by Gail Ravnitzky Silberglied ; illustrations by Michael Balderrama.
       p. cm.
  Includes index.
  ISBN 978-1-933253-36-7 (alk. paper)
  1. Museums--Public relations--United States. I. Balderrama, Michael, ill.
II. American Association of Museums. III. Title. IV. Title: American Association of Museums guide to advocacy.
  AM124.S55 2011
  069'.68--dc22
                          2011003211

Table of Contents

Acknowledgements

As a staffer on Capitol Hill for more than a decade, I met with hundreds of constituent groups. Many meetings were memorable, some for the wrong reasons. But all of them were important because people were participating in democracy. I always knew that my next career would be finding ways to better connect constituents with their elected officials, and I am grateful to be doing this work for the American Association of Museums.

First and foremost, to my talented and hardworking Government Relations colleagues, Carla J. Myers and Ember Farber: thank you for your expert advice, thoughtful suggestions, and overall support for this project. I am honored to work with you, and could not ask for a better team (I could perhaps ask for a bigger team, but certainly not a better one!).

And a very special thank-you to AAM President Ford Bell for his steadfast trust in me. Best boss ever.

Thank you to my colleagues at AAM, especially John Strand, publisher of The AAM Press, who provided expert guidance and support, Susan Levine, whose graphic design makes everything AAM does look gorgeous, and Sarah Parsons, Phil Katz, Monika Graves, Eileen Goldspiel, Patrick Gossett, Elizabeth Merritt, Andrea Jacob, Cecelia Walls, Kathy Maxwell, Lauren

Silberman, and Ariana Carella, who provided input and advice for this book. Thanks to Government Relations Interns Mike Balderrama and Kate Gaskill, who conducted helpful research, and to Mike for his creative illustrations. And to everyone else who makes AAM an interesting and fun place to work.

Thank you to those who reviewed sections of this book: April Carson, Counsel, Alliance for Justice, and David Thompson, Vice President of Public Policy, National Council of Nonprofits. Thank you to everyone who agreed to be quoted in this book, and to Tim Hysom, Director of The Partnership for a More Perfect Union, and Rhonda Richards, a former Senate Subcommittee Staff Director, who each provided valuable input. Thank you to the AAM Board of Directors, and to Lisa Vecoli and David Lebedoff for providing advice on getting board members involved in advocacy. Thank you to one of the smartest and most resourceful people I know, my brother Michael Ravnitzky, who also served as an expert reviewer, and to my devoted mom, Karleen Heller, who also happens to be an eagle-eyed proofreader.

The more I learn about museums, the more I love them. I wish as a Hill staffer I had known how museums were addressing complex social issues in creative ways, and how museums were helping to teach the school curriculum. I wish I had known how museums brought cultural diplomacy abroad, and how much they contributed to local economies. Come to think of it, I wish I had known that aquariums, arboretums, historic homes, nature centers, planetariums, presidential libraries, public gardens, and zoos were, in fact, museums. Sure, I had plenty of other issues on my plate, but I wish there had been a Museums Advocacy Day so I could have learned more. Thank you to everyone who believed in—and continues to support—Museums Advocacy Day.

To the exceptional museum field—especially the national, state, and regional museum associations—that welcomed me, questioned me, trusted me, collaborated with me, helped me, inspired me, and continues to teach me,

I offer my humble thanks. And to everyone who makes our museum advocacy efforts successful—and to all who will make them even more successful in the future (i.e., you!)—I share my most heartfelt thanks.

And finally, thank you to one of the biggest museum supporters I know: my husband Steve. He not only served as an informal editor on this book, but also provided much support, patience, and love. If Museums Advocacy Day ever becomes a day for both the public and the museum field to advocate together, I know that Steve will be the first to register. And to my children, Jeremy, Jamie and Evan, who make me laugh out loud and make me immensely proud, who tire me and inspire me, and who always remind me of what's most important.

Gail Ravnitzky Silberglied

Preface

By Ford W. Bell

There are so many valuable things that museums do on behalf of our communities. We educate and inspire. We preserve and interpret the past, help to make sense of the present, and work to prepare a better, more sustainable future.

But our ability to accomplish all this and much more might be in jeopardy if we do not develop our skills at one essential task: advocacy.

In this wonderful new book by AAM's Director of Government Relations, Gail Ravnitzky Silberglied, advocacy is defined broadly, as it should be. We advocate for the value of our museums every time we open an exhibit, welcome a school group, send out a press release, meet with funders or hold a special event for the community. Advocacy can be as simple and personal as chatting with a visitor. We have the opportunity to do it every day, in many different ways. It is an essential task for everyone in the museum, from paid and volunteer staff to boards of trustees.

Advocacy is also the more complex task of interacting with our elected officials at all levels of government, from the local school board to the U.S. Senate. This book demystifies that task, offering a rich array of smart and practical advice that can turn any of us into an effective and convincing advocate in any situation, before any audience, whether around the corner or in the halls of Congress.

We in museums need this book. The truth is, we are late to this effort. Our profession has a long way to go in learning how to advocate for itself effectively and with a unified voice. Our esteemed colleagues in the library field, for example, have been good at advocacy on the local, state and national levels for decades. AAM held its first Museums Advocacy Day in Washington in 2009. Thanks to the efforts of many dedicated people, it has now become an annual event. But we have some catching up to do.

My hope is that everyone in the museum profession will read this book, absorb its lessons, follow its advice and work at becoming good advocates. But I hold out greatest hope for the newest members of our field, the students and recent graduates, the emerging museum professionals who represent a new generation of advocates. They are the ones who must create and lead real change: a true, field-wide advocacy, effective and committed, that will become an integral part of our work, as natural to us as educating a visitor, interpreting a collections object or telling a story.

This book helps us take a major step in that direction. From all of us at AAM: read and enjoy!

Ford W. Bell, DVM
President, AAM

ad·vo·ca·cy [AD-vuh-kuh-see], n.
The act of pleading for, supporting, or recommending.

Introduction

Want to learn how to be a great advocate? Guess what. You already are!

It's true. You advocate all the time. You might be asking a donor to make a major gift. Or you might be asking your local paper to write about your new exhibit. On a simpler, personal level, you might be negotiating with a friend or spouse about which movie to see.

Every time you make your case, no matter what the topic, you are being an advocate.

Museums often have a coordinated strategy for advocating to donors, or for reaching out to the public. But when it comes to making our case to elected officials, the museum field can—and must—do much more.

Sure, advocating to elected officials can be a little intimidating. You might feel they are too busy. Or you might assume they support museums and don't need to hear from you.

In fact, as a constituent you have the right—and the responsibility—to educate elected officials about what is going on in your community. Are you sure they know about the economic impact that museums have? Do you think they already know that museums are partnering with the public school system to help teach the local curriculum?

This book is designed to help you feel confident in using your existing advocacy skills to support museums at all levels of government, from the local town council to the U.S. Senate. You already advocate to other audiences: donors, the media, and the public. After reading this book, we hope you will be able to comfortably advocate to one more key audience: your elected officials.

Why must we make our case to legislators? Consider what they face: a $1.3 trillion federal budget deficit, a $14 trillion national debt, and a steady stream of constituents, each bringing a carefully crafted, compelling request. Lawmakers and their staffs must sort through dozens of issues, thousands of emails and letters, and billions of dollars worth of spending decisions. It's easy for museums to be overlooked.

The fact that elected officials have so many issues on their plates is all the more reason to educate them about what you do. If you don't tell them, who will?

Consider the example of the 2009 economic stimulus bill.

In January 2009, Congress began considering legislation to deal with the sudden and devastating economic downturn. The goals were to create jobs and invest in our nation's infrastructure. Late one night we learned some alarming news. The House legislation would include language barring zoos and aquariums from competing for any of the funds. The ban also included casinos, golf courses, and swimming pools. The museum field asked: How could this happen? How do we stop this?

How did museums get targeted this way? It all started with a polar bear.

As the bill was being crafted, the U.S. Conference of Mayors identified $19 billion in potential "shovel ready" projects (remember that term?) that would put people to work right away. Not surprisingly, museums were frequently listed. Mayors understood that museums are economic anchors in the community. Mayors understand that museums drive tourism.

One such project was identified by the city of Providence, Rhode Island: a new polar bear exhibit at the Providence Zoo.

Some people jumped on this proposed exhibit as a blatant example of "wasteful spending." Congress reacted by seeking a way to avoid such criticism.

With $825 billion at stake, the museum community began to mobilize.

In cooperation with the Association of Zoos and Aquariums, AAM sent Advocacy Alerts to the museum field. As a result, thousands of letters and emails poured in to Capitol Hill. We made our case: "This is a complete misunderstanding of the vital role that zoos and aquariums—and other museums and historic sites—play in our society and the role they will play in the economic recovery."

When the U.S. Senate first took up the bill, it did not include such a provision. But Senator Tom Coburn (R-OK) prepared a series of amendments. They were all bad news for museums.

The Senate debated and voted on this amendment: "None of the amounts appropriated or otherwise made available by this Act may be used for any casino or other gambling establishment, aquariums, zoo, golf course, swimming pool, stadium, community park, museum, theater, art center and highway beautification project."

We were outraged! Now museums were banned from competing for these funds, too.

Despite a massive grassroots campaign, this amendment passed by a vote of 73-24, proving that museums were fundamentally misunderstood on Capitol Hill. Museums were seen as nice but not necessary. They weren't considered job creators. They weren't seen as essential.

Once the House and Senate passed their versions of the bills, a Conference Committee met to sort out differences between the two versions. This was our chance. The museum field kept the pressure on. Billions of dollars were being negotiated and all we asked for was the deletion of three words: museums, zoos and aquariums. Simply put, we asked that museums, zoos and aquariums be allowed to compete for economic stimulus funds.

We created an online form on the AAM website to help museums quickly and easily send Economic Impact Statements to Capitol Hill. The message: Yes, we do stimulate the economy. We employ people. We support local businesses. We attract critical tourism dollars. Museums are essential economic assets.

As the House and Senate versions were being reconciled, we got daily—and sometimes hourly—updates on where things stood in the battle. For a while it was touch and go. But we kept up the pressure.

At last, victory. The amendment was altered. We got what we had advocated for—but only in part. While we were able to get the word "museum" removed from the amendment, zoos and aquariums remained. Try as we might, we could not get them to remove these last two words. It was a bittersweet victory.

In a way, this was a wake-up call for the larger museum field, a fire drill of sorts. And fortunately we survived this time, albeit by the skin of our teeth.

It's really insulting when you think about it. Forget all the people employed at zoos and aquariums. Forget all the environmental education and wildlife conservation. And forget all the local tourism dollars that zoos and aquariums attract. They were to be shut out of federal stimulus funds by this bill.

The law of the land would include this: "None of the funds appropriated or otherwise made available in this Act may be used by any State or local government, or any private entity for any casino or other gambling establishment, aquarium, zoo, golf course, or swimming pool."

In a nice touch of irony, President Obama signed the economic stimulus bill into law at the Denver Museum of Nature and Science. The museum has 465 solar panels on its roof, and was chosen as the event site to highlight the importance of developing alternative energy sources and green jobs.

With a tough economic climate and new political realities, we are likely to see more examples of how museums are poorly understood, ignored and unappreciated by some lawmakers. Outstanding advocacy efforts of the museum field saved the day this time. Next time…?

We need to work together to make sure that never again do 74 U.S. senators vote against the interests of museums.

Nonprofits "generally are permitted to engage in advocacy or lobbying related to their exempt purposes."

—U.S. Internal Revenue Service

Chapter 2

What Is Allowed and What Is Not?

"I'm not allowed to advocate."

I hear this all the time, and it's just not true.

No matter what type of organization you work for, you can still find a way to be an advocate for museums.

If you work for a private 501(c)(3) nonprofit—and that is most of you—the U.S. Internal Revenue Service explicitly preserves your right to advocate on behalf of your museum and its mission.

Sure, there are rules that nonprofit organizations must follow, but the rules are not complicated. We have created this guide to help you distinguish between what is allowed and what is not.

In this chapter, we are discussing nonprofit organizations, which are tax-exempt, 501(c)(3) organizations (an Internal Revenue Service designation). These account for 99 percent of institutions in the museum field. Chances are, the following rules apply to you and your organization.

Let's start with the one exception: If you work for a museum that is operated by the city, state, or federal government, you may have restrictions on what you are allowed to do on company time.

But have no fear: you did not give up your citizenship when you accepted your job.

During my time on Capitol Hill, constituents came in regularly and mentioned their current job and made it clear that they were visiting Congress as private citizens. This is all perfectly legitimate.

Here's how you go about it:

"My name is Jane Smith. I am employed as a Curator at the Johnson County Museum, but I am here in a private capacity as one of your constituents because I care about museums."

And then you make your case.

Some of you might still be thinking, "But I'm not allowed to *lobby*!" Let's clear up the difference between advocacy and lobbying.

Advocacy occurs when you make the case for museums, broadly. **Lobbying** is one form of advocacy and usually involves an attempt to influence legislation.

As a 501(c)(3), you are allowed to do both.

Even if you are the most dedicated advocate for museums (and if you are, thank you!), you probably don't come close to spending a substantial portion of your time on lobbying activities. If you do spend a substantial amount of time advocating for museums (again, thank you!), you may consider filling out a one-page form for the IRS. It's called a "501(h) election," and it helps you determine exactly how much you can spend, based on your budget size. For the vast majority of museums, this is probably not necessary. *For more information on the rules around lobbying and advocacy, we recommend contacting the Alliance for Justice at* www.afj.org.

Now that we have cleared that up, let's look at what you are allowed to do.

As a nonprofit organization, your museum receives certain tax benefits. With these advantages comes the requirement that you not participate in any partisan activities or appear to support or oppose political candidates. But there is plenty that you *can* do.

Here's the scoop:

YES, you can!	NO, you can't
Participate in a campaign on your own time	Use office computers, supplies, telephones, email, fax, or other resources for partisan political activity
Host a candidates forum	Invite only your preferred candidate(s) or discuss only a single issue
Be an enthusiastic supporter of a particular candidate	Wear candidate t-shirts or buttons in your museum or at official events
Decorate your home or apartment with campaign or candidate-related items	Decorate your office space with items that can be perceived as supporting or opposing particular candidates or political parties
Do voter education: help inform voters about issues in an election	Tell people whom to vote for
Do voter registration: help register people to vote	Register only those who agree with you

YES, you can!	NO, you can't
Do get-out-the-vote activities	Tell people whom to vote for
Allow a candidate to rent your space for a campaign event (at fair-market value)*	Only allow certain candidates to rent the space, donate your space, or provide a discounted rate
Donate personal funds	Make an organizational monetary or in-kind donation
Volunteer on your personal time	Volunteer on company time
Make candidates aware of your organization's agenda	Ask candidates to endorse your organization's agenda
Publicize Election Day	List information favorable to a particular candidate
Ask all candidates to fill out a questionnaire about issues	Ask only some candidates to fill out a questionnaire about issues
Work on behalf of a ballot measure: for example, a ballot initiative to set aside 1% of a sales tax for cultural organizations	Spend more than a substantial amount of time or money working on a ballot measure**

*Some museums will not do this because they wish to avoid the appearance of impropriety, but it is allowed.

** For more information on the rules around lobbying and advocacy, we recommend contacting the Alliance for Justice at www.afj.org.

Nonprofits have an important civic role to play on Election Day. Here's what you can and cannot do to get involved:

YES, you can!	NO, you can't
Encourage your staff to vote	Tell them whom to vote for
Allow late arrival/early departure for voting	Allow late arrival/early departure for campaign work
Allow staff to serve as a nonpartisan election worker on company time	Allow staff to participate in a political campaign on company time
Include Election Day as an organization-wide holiday	Make people participate in election day activities
Use personal leave time to participate in campaigns	Make your staff participate in a campaign
Provide information on early and absentee voting, location of polling places, ID requirements, and links to candidate information	Present any of this information in a partisan way
Congratulate re-elected or newly elected officials	Characterize it in a partisan way (i.e., declare it a "victory for our issues")

If your museum becomes involved in nonpartisan, election-related activities, it increases the possibility that someone—either on your staff or elsewhere—will make a mistake and cross the line between what is allowed and what is not.

Here are a few things to consider when dealing with elected officials, and a few things you can do to protect your museum's interests:

- Make sure your employees, board members, and volunteers are aware of the restrictions on partisan activities. You may want to circulate this information or hold a training session.

- Require all employees, board members, and volunteers to state clearly that they are acting in their individual capacity, not on company time and not on behalf of the organization, when they engage in partisan political activity. Any reference to the organization is made for identification purposes only.

- Become aware of the difference between working with an elected official's office for an official event (a community town hall, for example) vs. a campaign event. There are times when the confusion is caused by the elected official's own staff. I've seen it happen.

- If you notice that an event has created an appearance of partisan activity, you should take immediate corrective action. For example, if a political campaign wishes to hold a campaign event at your museum, it may appear that your museum is endorsing that candidate. By simply making it clear that your facilities are available to everyone on the same basis, you can set the record straight.

- Always request and maintain documentation about any political events that take place at your museum.

By now it should be clear that you are, in fact, allowed to be an advocate. And you are allowed to lobby, too.

Now, I can understand if you don't want to use the word "lobbyist," because, well, we lobbyists get a bad rap—even if we are lobbying for museums!

But someone has to do it.

And more of us need to.

Special thanks to Alliance for Justice (www.afj.org) and Independent Sector (www.independentsector.org) for being valuable resources on this topic.

"Be Prepared."

–Girl Scout and Boy Scout Motto

Chapter 3

An Advocacy Inventory

Before you reach out to a potential donor, you do your homework, right?

You find out his personal and philanthropic interests, his ability to give, his giving history, and his connections to your board members and to other people you know. You do all this to craft just the right message.

Next, you don't just ask for money, but you seek to develop stronger and deeper ties with the donor, in hopes of increasing his gifts over time. You find out why he supports your museum. You ask for his support on efforts you know will be of special interest to him. You keep him posted about what your museum is up to. You know that building these relationships takes a lot of time and effort, but you also know it is valuable in the long term.

The same principles apply to cultivating relationships with elected officials.

In order to make your case effectively, you will need to create a concise, compelling message. You need examples, and you need facts.

What you *don't* need is to conduct extensive research. You already have all the information you need: in your annual report, in your brochure, on your museum's tax return (for nonprofits, Form 990) and perhaps on your museum's website.

We created an Advocacy Inventory to help you get started.

Remember, these are just suggestions for information you may wish to collect. You will find some sections more useful and relevant than others. The inventory is designed to be an arsenal of information that you can use when opportunities arise.

We should also make it clear up front that responsibility for the Advocacy Inventory should not be left to one person alone.

It is a perfect activity, however, for your board of directors to work on together during a board meeting.

It can also be done as a case study for a graduate class in museum studies.

(You can download and print this document at www.speakupfor museums.org/advocacyinventory.)

Part I: About Your Museum

Annual budget: _____

Amount of taxes paid in community: _____

Amount of tax revenue generated in the community: _____

Number of employees: _____

Number of volunteers: _____

Number of volunteer hours:_____

Number of members/supporters:_____

List of states, counties, cities, and towns served: _____

_____

Admission fee, if any: _____

Number of visitors each year:_____

Number (or percentage) of out of town visitors each year:_____

Number of educators that participated in teacher training programs: _____

Special community groups served (seniors, veterans, at-risk teens, military families, international visitors, etc.): _____

_____

Number of schools participating in class trips: _____

List of schools participating in class trips:_____

_____

School districts served:_____

_____

Number of visits by schoolchildren each year: _____

Curriculum topics taught in cooperation with local school system: _____

_____

Funding (% by government, % by individuals, etc.): _____

_____

Government grants (how much, from where, what it has been used for, use outcomes if available, etc.): _____

_____

Diversity of museum visitors:_____

_____

Diversity of museum staff and trustees:_____

_____

Special outreach: _____

_____

Part II: Identifying Your Elected Officials

Mayor: _____

Members of County Commission: _____

Members of Town Council:_____

Members of City Council:_____

Members of Tribal Council: _____

Governor: _____

State Representative(s): _____

State Senator(s):_____

U.S. Representative: _____

U.S. Senator:_____

U.S. Senator:_____

Head, State Department of Education: _____

Director, relevant statewide offices (e.g., Cultural Affairs, Arts Commission, Historic Preservation Office, etc.):_____

Local School Superintendent: _____

Members of the School Board:_____

Others: _____

Part III: Lifecycle of Elected Bodies

In Congress, there is an annual appropriations process, during which every part of the federal government is funded. The process begins in February when the president proposes a budget. Then members of Congress begin to circulate "Dear Colleague" letters, in which they ask other Members of Congress to join them in supporting the programs that are most important to them. Hearings are held in March and April, and then the House Appropriations Committee begins writing a series of bills to fund each part of the government. Over the summer, the House and Senate consider each of these bills and numerous amendments, then reconcile any differences. The process is supposed to be completed by the end of the fiscal year, September 30.

While it rarely happens exactly like this, it is a good outline of how the process works. Knowing this give us the opportunity, for example, to encourage members of Congress to sign on to the Dear Colleague letter in support of funding for the Institute of Museum and Library Services Office of Museum Services. And we submit a letter in December requesting that AAM be permitted to testify before Congress during the hearing process.

At the state and local level, you can maximize your effectiveness by knowing the process and weighing in at the right time. Much of this information is available online through state or local government websites.

There is nothing worse than having a compelling request that cannot be acted upon because you went in a few months too late. Capturing all or even some of this information will help you time your outreach effectively.

Here's a hint to get you started: If you don't know the answer to these questions (and why would you? There's a lot to keep track of), give your elected officials a call and ask! Their staffs will likely be happy to help you, and then you can send a thank you note and begin to build the relationship.

State Legislature:

When is the legislature in session? _____

What is the budget cycle? _____

Is there time set aside for public witness testimony? _____

If so, when?_____

How do you go about being considered for testimony? _____

County Commission:

When is the commission in session?_____

What is the budget cycle? _____

Is there time set aside for public witness testimony? _____

If so, when?_____

How do you go about being considered for testimony? _____

City/Town/Tribal Council:

When is the council in session?_____

What is the budget cycle? _____

Is there time set aside for public witness testimony? _____

If so, when?_____

How do you go about being considered for testimony? _____

Part IV: Gathering the Facts

Next you should identify a few elected officials with whom you want to develop or strengthen your museum's relationship. As in previous sections, some of the information may not be relevant, but it will be helpful to have in your arsenal.

Name of Elected Official #1:

Title: _____

Areas represented: _____

Length of time in office:_____

Previous experience/jobs held:_____

_____

Hometown:_____

Education: _____

Family connections:_____

5 top policy interests:_____

_____

Has your museum worked with him/her? (This could include meetings,

　　phone calls, visits to your museum, attendance at events, etc.)　If so,

　　on what topic(s)? _____

_____

If so, do you have staff contact information? _____

Does anyone on your board or staff have a personal connection to this

　　elected official?_____

In what capacity? _____

Name of Elected Official #2:

　　Title: _____

　　Areas represented: _____

　　Length of time in office:_____

　　Previous experience/jobs held:_____

_____

Hometown: _____

Education: _____

    Family connections: _____

    5 top policy interests: _____

    _____

    Has your museum worked with him/her? (This could include meetings,

        phone calls, visits to your museum, attendance at events, etc.)   If so,

        on what topic(s)? _____

    _____

    If so, do you have staff contact information? _____

    Does anyone on your board or staff have a personal connection to this

        elected official? _____

    In what capacity? _____

Name of Elected Official #3:

    Title: _____

    Areas represented: _____

    Length of time in office: _____

    Previous experience/jobs held: _____

    _____

    Hometown: _____

    Education: _____

    Family connections: _____

5 top policy interests:_____

_____

Has your museum worked with him/her? (This could include meetings,
  phone calls, visits to your museum, attendance at events, etc.) If so,
  on what topic(s)? _____

_____

If so, do you have staff contact information? _____

Does anyone on your board or staff have a personal connection to this
  elected official?_____

In what capacity? _____

Part V: Gathering Testimonials/Stories

Consider whether you have "success stories" about members of the community whose lives have been transformed by a visit to your museum. If
your museum were asked to testify, whom might you call upon to speak
about the value and importance of your museum?

Do you have letters from schoolchildren or their teachers? Do you have testimonials from veterans? From children with special needs and their families?
From seniors? From international visitors? From someone who pursued an
education or a professional career after being inspired at your museum?

Perhaps you can call upon your volunteers to talk about why they volunteer
and why they love your museum. Some will have terrific stories about how
the museum has had a positive influence on visitors or on the community
as a whole.

You might even have elected officials who have been longtime supporters of
your museum. Have they ever made a public statement about your

museum? Did they send you a letter of congratulations after visiting one of your new exhibits, or on another of your museum's accomplishments?

Gathering these stories and testimonials will be valuable. You never know when they may be useful to help make your case to an elected official. Not to get all mushy here, but it will also reaffirm all the things that make you proud of your museum!

Part VI: Making Connections

At the end of this exercise, you will have all the tools you need to make connections between your elected officials and the work you do.

Perhaps you learned that an elected official grew up in a town where your museum is very involved with the school district. Perhaps you learned that an elected official is very interested in energy efficiency, in which case you would want to emphasize your energy efficiency efforts and what else you want to accomplish in this area. Perhaps you learned that an elected official was a history teacher, in which case you can focus on the history lessons you impart to local school kids. The key is making that special connection on a personal or professional level.

You won't use all of this information with every elected official. But you will have a robust arsenal of information that you can use to craft the most compelling and individualized case for each of them.

It is important to note that these connections may not be obvious. For the purposes of this exercise, it is important to think broadly. The great thing about museums is that there really is something for everyone. Here are a few examples:

At a local historical society, you can learn about the family genealogy of the area's original settlers and early farmers, crafts makers and business people.

Any connection here to some of your elected officials?

Several art museums have art therapy or art education programs designed for families dealing with the crushing effects of Alzheimer's disease. If one of your legislators happens to sit on a committee that oversees health care issues, this would be a terrific connection to make.

At the National Baseball Hall of Fame and Museum in Cooperstown, New York, you can learn about geography, history, civil rights, economics, leadership, popular culture, special abilities, labor history, mathematics, fine art, women's history, industrial technology, science, and cultural diversity—not to mention batting averages! This is a great example of the breadth of museum collections, showing how one artifact or exhibition topic leads to a whole range of related issues.

What might your elected officials be surprised to learn about your museum?

I had the privilege of serving for almost 30 years as a trustee/ director of museums in my home state of Minnesota. Because of that important experience, and my years on the job here at AAM, I have come to believe that it is critically important for museum trustees to be aware of, and engaged in, the issues that are of paramount importance to the broader museum field.

– Ford W. Bell, DVM, President, American Association of Museums

Chapter 4

Your Secret Weapon: Your Board

We've already discussed the many ways in which advocacy directed at elected officials is very much like the work you do to cultivate donors and engage the public.

It's all about pairing the most effective spokesperson with the most effective message.

Board Members are in the perfect position to help carry your message to elected officials. Here's why:

1. They know people. They have established networks and connections, and may already have an existing relationship with your elected officials. You probably already call upon board members to help with fundraising. Advocacy in this context is about taking similar messages to another audience: elected officials.

2. They have a different kind of authority. Museum professionals are perfectly capable of being effective advocates, but board members have

something even more powerful. Because they often come from a different industry and may be employed elsewhere, they are seen as more independent, and can act as "third-party validators."

3. They bring a different perspective. Chances are your board is made up of people with divergent backgrounds, varying philosophies, and different approaches (which may make for some really interesting meetings!). You may have educators, business leaders, veterans, philanthropists, community leaders and parents on your board. All of these perspectives may help make the case for your museum in a new, more influential way. This approach may be more appealing to an elected official.

4. They bring diversity. It's likely that your board already reflects the diversity of the communities you serve. This is already important in your public outreach efforts. It can also be valuable for advocating to elected officials, especially when your museum is serving more isolated or underserved communities.

5. They bring geographic diversity. Depending on where you live, you may have board members living in several different states, or several different counties. Therefore they have the ability to reach out to many more elected officials—as constituents—than you could by yourself.

6. They are considered experts. It is assumed that everyone associated with your museum is fairly well versed in all that the museum does. But there is an expectation that board members will also have access to different kinds of information: structural, financial, and organizational. This doesn't mean that they must memorize your tax return. Rather, they can simply carry the message with extra authority. They may have institutional knowledge about a particular topic, or simply have a breadth of experience from years of work in museums or in another field. Just as your museum staff holds its board members in high esteem, so will your community.

7. They put their money where their mouths are. There is an assumption that your trustees have weighed the many competing priorities in their lives and decided to invest in your museum. By contributing their time, energy, and money to your museum's cause, they are making a subtle yet powerful statement that your museum deserves public support.

8. They (may) have more time. Some of your board members may be retired. Some may have a lot of flexibility in their schedules. And some may view their board responsibilities as a welcome distraction from their other work.

9. They may be aligned politically. The good news for museums is that there is no niche constituency: the fact is, everyone loves museums! However, there may be some elected officials who are more or less inclined to support your museum based on political considerations. If the elected official is a fiscal conservative, for example, he or she may not support your public funding. Finding the right messenger—perhaps a board member who has a financial or corporate background—can help overcome these concerns. In this case, this board member can discuss the museum as a wise economic investment for the community.

I think we've made our point.

But now what? How do we go about getting board members to advocate for museums?

The first thing is to realize that you already rely on board members to serve as "ambassadors" for your museum: to donors, to community groups, to the media. Extending this ambassador role to advocacy is not really such a stretch.

One strategy is to involve your board in an advocacy exercise. In chapter 3, we recommended having your board conduct an "Advocacy Inventory" to enhance and centralize your arsenal of information that you use to advocate.

An Advocacy Inventory will help your board members identify natural connections between them and your elected officials.

Some of your board members may already have connections to local elected officials, and may be willing to expand these connections and reach out to elected officials on the state or federal level.

Another strategy is to keep your board up to date on what's happening on the advocacy front. You know what they say: "Out of sight, out of mind." So keep them aware of what's going on.

One way to do this is to always include an Advocacy Update on your board meeting agenda. A board member can even be assigned to report on this topic. Does your board have an Advocacy Committee? Maybe it should.

If you yourself are a board member reading this and want to get more involved (first of all, thank you!), think about the small steps you can take right away. Will you volunteer to provide an advocacy report at board meetings? Will you encourage your board to complete an Advocacy Inventory during an upcoming board meeting? Will you attend Museums Advocacy Day?

To further engage your board, we recommend making sure they all receive AAM's Advocacy Alerts (you can sign up to receive them right away by visiting www.speakupformuseums.org). That way, during board meetings, you can discuss the latest Advocacy Alerts and be sure your museum is getting involved at all the right times.

AAM works hard to provide clear and concise messages to advocates and to provide a specific "ask" in our Advocacy Alerts. We know that this makes advocacy so much easier! There's nothing worse than contacting elected officials with an unclear message, only to have them say (or think), "Now what do these people want me to do?"

AAM's advocacy website, www.speakupformuseums.org, also makes advocacy very easy, with contact information for legislators and with template letters that can be personalized and sent electronically.

One last strategy is to involve the board in all of your advocacy activities. This is particularly helpful for board members who may be intimidated by advocacy, or for the smaller museum with a lower profile. Invite board members to join you if you attend a public hearing. If you invite elected officials to visit your museum, invite a few board members to be present. As they get more involved in advocacy activities, they will feel more comfortable and you will have new advocacy surrogates that you can turn to.

To further build their confidence in advocacy, be sure that all board members are equipped with information, statistics, and success stories about your museum, so that they are always ready to advocate for your museum.

Building relationships is key to everything your museum does. The same principle holds true for elected officials. The more you learn about them, the better position you are in to be an effective advocate. You can follow elected officials on Twitter, or become a fan on Facebook. And if they leave office, don't count them out. Maintain these relationships, too, since you never know when someone will re-emerge on the political scene in a new capacity.

At some point, you may even invite an elected official (or a former one) to serve on your board. If you pursue this route, consider what kinds of activities or board committees that you would want them to become involved in. One way they can be extremely helpful is in creating a strategy for contacting other elected officials.

However you choose to involve your board members in advocacy, the basic case for museums must always be crystal clear: museums are *essential*.

- They are economic engines.
- They are a critical part of the educational infrastructure.
- They create jobs.
- They are stewards of our national heritage.
- They foster creativity and innovation.
- They spur tourism.
- They help to revitalize communities.
- They celebrate cultural diversity.
- They attract businesses to the community.
- They serve as community anchors.
- They are a source of civic and community pride.

These facts must be made clear to every elected official at every level of government.

And here's a final thought for you: advocacy is really a fundamental responsibility of all board members. AAM believes so strongly in this concept that it plans to add this tenet to its official "job description" of a board member. Perhaps your board should, too!

"Never doubt that a small group of thoughtful, committed people can change the world. Indeed, it is the only thing that ever has."

—*Margaret Mead*

Chapter 5

Keys to Success: What You Need To Know To Advocate Successfully for Museums

When Senator Richard Durbin (D-IL) gave the keynote address at the 2010 Museums Advocacy Day Congressional Breakfast, he talked about his quest to create the Abraham Lincoln Presidential Library and Museum in Springfield, Ill. "By Senate terms," he said, "it happened in a heartbeat: 16 years."

Everyone laughed.

But the lessons were clear: the legislative process can be painfully slow, and persistence pays off. Working with elected officials also takes perseverance, patience and a thoughtful approach.

The good news is that, unless you plan to build a major, federally funded museum from scratch, it will not take anywhere near 16 years to see results when you begin working with elected officials!

It is, however, important to have the right tools at your disposal—the right attitude, the right message, and the right follow-through—to be an effective museum advocate.

That is what we are providing here: our best advice to ensure that your efforts are as successful as possible. Happy advocating!

Know Your Power. As a constituent, you have an enormous amount of influence. Your elected official wants to learn about what constituents think and how he or she can help. An elected official will avoid saying "no" whenever possible. It might mean you won't get a straight answer some of the time, but it is why being persistent can really pay off. The last thing an elected official wants to see is a bunch of unhappy constituents: he knows it may cost him his job.

Have the Right Attitude. It is good to keep in mind that your elected officials work for you. However, it is also important to recognize that elected officials must balance many competing priorities and make tough decisions. You may not agree on every issue, but it is vital to build and maintain the relationship over the long term. In fact, it is when you have disagreed on something that an elected official may be even more inclined to find a way to work with you on another issue. You always want to remain a trusted community resource.

Respect the Staff. Elected officials greatly rely on their staffs, so it is important to treat every member of the staff with respect. Staffers make recommendations about issues, manage interactions with the media and other community leaders, and arrange the elected official's schedule. They wield a lot of influence. They can often make things happen when you can't reach your elected official directly. They can make sure your event stays on the calendar when something else comes up. Another thing to keep in mind is that today's staff assistant may be tomorrow's legislative director, and today's legislative aide may run for office some day. (There are currently more than 100 members of Congress who have served at some point as staff for an elected official!) Managing these relationships properly is essential, and can even lead to having an internal champion for your cause among the staff.

Be Specific. With so many competing priorities, it is important to identify exactly what you are asking for, and to be as specific as possible. Whether you are asking an official to cosponsor a bill, co-sign a letter, offer an amendment, attend an event, or make a public statement, be sure to provide as many details as are available, and to make accepting the request as easy as possible. For example, rather than asking, "Do you support museums?" ask specifically, "Do you support increasing federal funding for museums?" Or even more specifically, "Will you sign Congressman X's Dear Colleague letter requesting an increase in federal funding for museums?" It's also okay if you have a relationship-building request, such as "We just wanted to introduce ourselves" or "We're just here to say thank you." Just be up front about it.

Understand Your Audience. Elected officials play many roles: they are legislators, salesmen, customer service representatives, diplomats, celebrities, and sometimes ideologues. They often have a specific issue that they care most about, and they all are aware that education is a key concern in their communities. They probably ran for office because they want to help their communities. They spend a lot of time trying to reach out to each constituency, often with a goal of having public events and office hours in each of the towns or counties they represent. You can learn more about your elected officials by completing an Advocacy Inventory (see Chapter 3).

Learn the Process. There are many ways to learn how elected officials operate. (Reading this book is a great start!) By receiving AAM's advocacy alerts, by participating in AAM's online advocacy training series and other in-person training sessions, and by becoming more involved in the process yourself, you can learn how and when it is best to weigh in. Because every office operates a little differently, it's okay to ask your elected officials how you can be most effective and what they expect will happen on a given issue—their staffs are usually happy to help! We have also provided a list of resources in Chapter 9 to help you become a veritable expert. Finally, we'd be remiss if we didn't also mention here that participating in our annual Museums Advocacy Day in Washington, DC, is a great way to get a crash course on the issues and learn how to be an effective advocate!

Be Polite. Elected officials often get an earful from constituents about a range of issues. A thank-you will always be appreciated, and will often be remembered. Saying thank you is also a good opportunity to remind elected officials of the issues you discussed and to follow up with any information you offered to provide. Even when you disagree, it is important to find a way to disagree respectfully, so you do not damage the long-term relationship.

Be Flexible. If you are meeting an elected official, understand that things may change at the last minute. You may have to meet with staff instead. You may end up having the meeting "on the go" while the elected official walks to another meeting. You may have to wait a few minutes—or longer—for an elected official to join the meeting. The meeting may have to be cut short due to a last-minute schedule change. All of this is normal and should be expected. While it may be disappointing, don't take any of it personally.

Develop Your "Elevator Speech." If you had just 30 seconds to introduce yourself and your museum to an elected official, would you know what to say? Would you talk about your latest exhibit? Would you mention the school districts that you work with to teach the local curriculum? Would you mention a grant you just received? There is not necessarily a right or wrong answer for what you should say, but it is a good thing to think about in advance so you don't feel afterward that you missed an opportunity to make the case you really want to make.

Be Honest. If you are asked a question and do not know the answer, the best strategy is to be honest. It is perfectly fine to say, "I don't know but I will find out." Some people might feel embarrassed by such a situation, but try to think of it this way: It can actually be a positive turn of events, because now you have a terrific excuse to follow up! Besides, your reputation is everything, so be sure your information is always correct. If you find out later that something you said wasn't entirely correct, you should always provide the more updated information as quickly as possible.

Be Concise. Considering how much information an elected official has to sort through on any given day, it is best to provide a one-page summary of your issue. It is helpful to add information at the end indicating where they can find more details, or offer to provide it if they ask. You may be very proud of your latest 28-page annual report, but an elected official is unlikely to have time to do more than flip through it, if that.

Be Prepared. It is important to do some basic research about your elected officials. This will help you understand their priorities, which will help you craft your message. Know their committee assignments so you know what issues they spend more time working on. It may seem obvious, but read their bios (usually found on their websites) and look at recent press releases before your visit. Being prepared is so important that we cover this more extensively in Chapter 3.

Follow Up. If you promised to provide additional information, send it right away. If you didn't know the answer to a question, be sure to send the information as soon as possible. Even if you had a meeting where no specific follow up is needed, be sure to follow up just to say thank you. It is perfectly acceptable during a meeting to ask when they might reach a decision about your request. Then you'll know exactly when to follow up!

Be Newsworthy. Elected officials usually love the spotlight and they often enjoy being part of events that will be covered by the media. Consider what you have that is "the original," "the first," or "the largest." Will your museum be celebrating an anniversary or milestone? Is there a prominent person involved with your museum? Is there an interesting visual? Are you providing a solution to a community problem? If you can share this kind of information early on, the elected official may have ideas about how to promote the newsworthy event—and himself or herself in the process. Reporters and assignment editors are always looking for what they call the "news hook," and will also appreciate advance notice of such events.

Remember Why You Are There. When meeting an elected official, people can get very distracted, and sometimes they even leave the meeting without raising their issue. This might sound implausible, but it happens. Your elected official might want to reminisce about his or her experience in your museum, talk about local issues, or tell you about something he or she is working on. This is all great, but be sure you have a chance to make your request.

Be a Squeaky Wheel. Elected officials have numerous requests coming their way on a regular basis, so it can be easy to get lost in the crowd. Always let them know you'll be following up with them, and then do so.

Be Memorable. Your meeting with elected officials might be just one of many they have that day, so it's important to try to be memorable. Arranging to have the meeting take place at your museum is ideal, although that isn't always possible. In any case, it is important to try to make an impression (preferably a positive one!). When one small historic house museum testified to the state legislature, museum supporters arrived in costume. Perhaps you have an object from your collection that you could bring to a meeting with an elected official. Or simply bring a video clip of children visiting your museum. Making a splash can be very helpful, especially since getting on their radar can be half the battle!

Be a Storyteller. Statistics and hard facts are certainly important advocacy tools, but providing personal examples is a very powerful—and memorable—way to make your case. You can even collect testimonials from some of your museum's "success stories" so you can share your visitors' experiences in their own words. Here's one of my favorites: The Oregon Museum of Science and Industry proudly tells the story of an "OMSI kid" who built his first telescope at the museum. Today that kid is Dr. Michael Barratt, medical doctor and NASA astronaut, who joined the international space station in 2009. His connection to OMSI is so strong that he carried OMSI memorabilia with him on his space mission.

Be a Resource. Studies show that museums are one of society's most trusted institutions. This authority, combined with your persistent relationship building, can make you a valuable resource to your elected official. An elected official's staff is always looking for individuals to turn to for expert advice on a range of topics. If something comes up relating to museums, wouldn't it be great if they turned to you?

Be Real. If you are a small struggling museum, don't sugarcoat it. Be sure to show them the dire condition of your collection, or the building infrastructure issues that you cannot afford to properly address. Show them any situation that you are concerned could grow into a safety hazard. Show them your storage area. Show them your peeling paint. Elected officials need real information—and real images—to help them understand what museums need to continue preserving our heritage and educating our communities.

Work in a Coalition. You may already have coalitions that you work with on exhibits or fundraising. Coalitions can also be very important as you advocate for museums. It strengthens your hand and underscores the fact that museums are an intrinsic part of the community. Consider who might be a natural partner with common interests, or think outside the box to form more broad-based coalitions. Elected officials will appreciate knowing that the museum community bands together, shares resources, etc. Keep in mind that the coalition may be quite informal—you can get started by simply inviting two or three local museum colleagues to join you at an elected official's "Coffee and Conversation" or similar public event.

Get to Know the Farm Team. Did you know that the incoming crop of Senators in 2011 included a former state representative, a county councilman, a governor, four U.S. Representatives, and a county executive? Future senators and governors will also come from the current pool of local elected officials, so try to get to know your elected officials at all levels.

Make No Assumptions. Your elected officials may have heard of your museum. They may even have visited. But it would be a mistake to assume that they are aware of all that you do. For example, your museum may be providing a safe educational place for kids to go while their parents are working extra shifts. Your museum might have inspired a youngster to stay in school. Your museum may be helping to educate people about our nation's rich heritage and diversity, teaching English as a second language, or teaching about protecting the environment. Elected officials love to tell stories about the wonderful things going on in their communities. Fair warning: your museum's work may wind up being cited by the elected official again and again!

Tailor Your Message. Once you've identified your elected official's priorities, tailor your message accordingly. If it is education, tell officials about how you work with local schools. If it is the environment, tell them about your greening initiatives. If it is fiscal discipline, tell them how many jobs your museum creates or the percent of your budget that comes from private donations or foundation support. If their passion is working on issues affecting seniors, tell them about your lifelong learning programs or opportunities for seniors to volunteer with your museum. You can almost always find a connection to an issue they are passionate about.

A final note about perhaps the two most important keys to success: patience and persistence. Elected officials have a lot on their plates. On any given day, a lawmaker might be visited by nurses, bankers, veterans returning from war, foster parents, medical researchers, or families dealing with Alzheimer's or autism. Constituents might be asking for immediate action on health care, public safety, homelessness, the national debt, the environment, national security, and much more. It could take a little extra energy, time or creativity to get on the elected official's radar screen. But always remember that museums have every right to a seat at the table because they are essential to our communities. If we don't make our case, who will?

"You don't have to see the whole staircase, just take the first step."

– Martin Luther King, Jr.

Chapter 6

Start Advocating Today!
A Week-by-Week Plan

It can be intimidating.

You might be thinking: Elected officials are busy. I don't want to bother them. They have a lot on their plates right now; and for that matter, so do I! I don't have time for advocacy.

Nice try.

Even if you are from a small museum with few staff (or no staff!), you can still advocate. Working with your board of directors, volunteers and others, you can get started right away.

If you approach it incrementally, perhaps it will seem more manageable. Commit to doing one thing each week to promote your museum to elected officials. Some of these activities will take just a few minutes. Do one that you have time for. Then another. Some will advance museums directly. Others will help you build a relationship over time. All of them are valuable.

Here are some ideas to get you started:

1. Visit AAM's advocacy website at www.speakupformuseums.org and find out who represents you in Congress and in your state legislature.

2. Add your elected officials to your mailing list.

3. Go to www.speakupformuseums.org to send a letter inviting your members of Congress to visit your museum. Or give them a call (ask for the staff person who handles the elected official's schedule). Don't forget to include their staffs in any invitations!

4. Get Free Online Advocacy Training. Not only does AAM offer free online advocacy training sessions, it also has an extensive library of previous training programs available on its advocacy website. Surely you can spare one hour to try one out. Visit www.speakupformuseums.org for more information.

5. Invite elected officials and their staffs to attend (or participate in) your "First Friday" or "Second Saturday" events. These already established community events are a great opportunity to introduce your museum to your elected officials.

6. Write a letter to congratulate newly elected (or re-elected) legislators. After an election you can reach newly elected officials through their campaign offices. Once they are sworn in, write to them in their new offices to introduce yourself and your museum. That way, you also get on *their* mailing lists.

7. Sign up for AAM Advocacy Alerts here: www.speakupformuseums.org.

8. Participate in Museums Advocacy Day! This two-day annual event in Washington, DC, brings together museum professionals and supporters for a day of advocacy training, a Capitol Hill reception, and a day of visits to Capitol Hill. Learn more on AAM's advocacy website, www.speakupformuseums.org.

9. Choose something unique that your museum is doing and write an opinion piece about it for a local paper. Send a copy to your elected officials.

10. When you learn about something an elected official has done in support of museums or other educational or cultural institutions, write a note to say thank you. And write about it in your newsletter. Then be sure to send your elected official a copy of the newsletter.

11. Find your elected officials on Facebook, Twitter, or other social media websites. Become a fan, a friend, or a follower so you can learn about their activities and priorities. If you haven't yet developed a social media presence, consider joining one of these social media sites. One thing to keep in mind, though, is that it will require someone to monitor these sites and post information on a regular basis. If your museum is not ready for an official social media presence, consider following your elected officials from your personal Facebook or Twitter account.

12. Gather testimonials. As mentioned in the Advocacy Inventory (Chapter 3), it is helpful to compile your "fan mail" and share it with elected officials. This may include letters from visitors, volunteers, local teachers, donors, parents, students, veterans, international visitors, or anyone else in your community.

13. Involve your trustees. Set aside time at your next board meeting to discuss how they would like to become more involved in advocacy for museums.

14. Research your elected officials on LinkedIn and through other online sources. You may find that you have connections you were not aware of (for example, if some of your supporters are linked to elected officials as former colleagues).

15. Help create accurate museum data by participating in research initiatives such as the AAM Museum Financial Information survey. The information collected is vital to demonstrating the value of museums to elected officials at all levels.

16. Encourage your visitors to write to Congress about their visit to your museum. You can do this easily by directing them to www.speakupfor museums.org, or setting up a computer kiosk where visitors can send messages to Congress right on the spot.

17. Aim for at least one photo of an elected official at your museum. This can be from a visit or from an official event held at the museum.

18. Align with field-wide ethics and standards and become accredited. AAM standards (*Standards and Best Practices for U.S. Museums*, The AAM Press) and ethics (*Code of Ethics for U.S. Museums*) are valuable tools to help you advocate for your museum. If your museum is accredited, you probably already highlight this information with donors. When your museum becomes accredited or re-accredited, tell your elected officials. They will likely want to celebrate this achievement by making a public statement, presenting a certificate, or otherwise honoring your museum. You might also point to your museum's accreditation status if your state or local funding is threatened. We've seen this at work, and it is highly effective to be able to point to the museum's strict adherence to field-wide standards and ethics as a measure of your museum's commitment to excellence. (For more on accreditation, visit the AAM website, www.aam-us.org.)

19. Say Thank You Again! If an elected official (or staff) came to your event, wrote a letter in support of a grant request, or otherwise helped the museum, tell everyone—and let your elected official know that you are spreading the word!

20. Consider what your public profile looks like—after all, that's where elected officials may go to find information about your museum. Google your museum's name. Visit Wikipedia. Is your museum listed? How complete and accurate is your listing? Are there programs or special outreach efforts that should be highlighted? The good news is that it is easy to make changes to your listing on Wikipedia. Google also has a simple process to update addresses and business hours. Most other websites are willing to make changes, if asked.

21. Plan a special visit for the local staff of the elected officials your museum serves. Call and ask for the staff person who handles museum issues. You might find that they don't have anyone identified (we find this to be the case on Capitol Hill all the time, so we usually ask for the person who handles education issues). If you want to invite the entire elected official's staff, ask for the person who runs the office—it could be the Staff Director, Chief of Staff, or District Director. Plan a behind-the-scenes tour or schedule the visit as a preview for a new exhibit. Or invite staff to observe a class trip so they can see how you serve students.

22. Consider inviting an elected official (or former elected official) to serve on your board of directors.

23. Connect with your local Convention and Visitors Bureau or tourism board, which could bring added visibility to your museum. Their goal is to bring visitors to your area, so make sure you are on their radar screen. Offer museum literature for the tourism board to display. Or arrange for your museum to be a stop on a walking tour.

24. Join forces with other museums in your community. Set up a meeting with other local museum staff to consider how you might advocate for museums as a group. This way you can compare notes about issues facing your museum and strategies for working with the elected officials who represent you. Perhaps you will plan a group visit to your elected officials. If you already work closely with the other museums in your community, this will be easy. If not, it will be a good way to start!

25. Have you received a government grant for your museum? Make sure your legislators know how critical those funds were and how the museum used them. If you received a grant from the federal Institute of Museum and Library Services, you can use the template on the AAM advocacy website to contact Congress and share information about your museum's IMLS grant. This helps set the stage for sustained—and hopefully *increased*—funding for the agency.

26. Gather letters from local school children. If your museum welcomes school classes, ask them to write letters to you about what they learned. These are very valuable advocacy tools. If you are visiting your elected officials, for example, you can bring copies of a few letters to emphasize the critical role your museum plays in educating the next generation. Or ask the students to contact their elected officials directly. AAM has a template letter on its advocacy website specifically designed for use by students.

27. Get to know your city and state cultural affairs staff (Office of Cultural Resources or State Humanities Office, for example), or other offices responsible for these issues. Ask to meet with them to introduce your museum and the services you provide. You can go to them, or invite them to take a VIP tour of your museum.

28. Visit the websites of your elected officials to find "Office Hours" or "Coffee and Conversation" types of events in your community. And then show up. Better yet, ask a board member to attend with you or in your place.

29. Ask how you can be helpful, or how you can be a resource to your elected officials, especially those who are newly elected. As you come to interact with elected officials more and more, you will be relied upon as someone they can turn to. A nice way to work with elected officials once you've established such a relationship is to ask how you can be helpful. Hopefully they won't just think of asking you to support their next election campaign (!) and will instead consider ways in which they can partner with your museum.

30. Does your museum have a blog? If so, write about public policy issues and mention your elected officials when appropriate. If you have met the elected official's staff, email them a link so they can see what you've written.

31. Develop and practice your elevator speech. Imagine you run into your elected official in the grocery store and you had 30 seconds to make your pitch. Would you be prepared?

32. Invite elected officials to exhibition openings. Your museum may already hold a VIP opening for major donors and community leaders. Elected officials will love the opportunity to get a sneak peak, and so will their staffs.

33. Connect with elected officials' websites. If your elected official has a section on the website entitled, "About this District," ask if he/she would consider mentioning or linking to your museum.

34. Provide posters or artifacts from your museum. Offer to loan elected officials a poster or artifact (that won't be damaged by doing so). In their offices, elected officials love to display posters and items that quintessentially represent their community.

35. Offer to host the Congressional Arts Competition. Many Members of Congress participate in an annual event where local high school students compete in a Congressional Arts Competition. A Member of Congress would likely be thrilled to hold this event at a local museum. They may even ask you to be part of the judging process!

36. Be a community meeting place. Can your museum be the location for a blood drive, a food drive, flu shots, toys for tots, or a polling place for an election? If so, reach out to the appropriate entity (American Red Cross, a local food bank, a community health clinic, Marine Toys for Tots Foundation, or the Board of Elections, etc.) to learn more.

37. Keep up with trends in the field by subscribing to the publications of the Center for the Future of Museums, an initiative of the American Association of Museums. This will provide valuable information to help make your case to elected officials who are trying to address society's most challenging issues. Visit www.futureofmuseums.org for more information.

38. Involve the families of elected officials. Spouses and children of elected officials provide yet another potential connection point for your museum. It is important to note that some spouses will shy away from public activities; others will enjoy them and even seek them out. Depending on the situation, you may want to add the spouse to your VIP outreach list, too, perhaps by using the home address. You can invite them to a special tour, exhibit opening, or a public program offered at your museum. Elected officials also may have children who would be inclined to get involved with your museum.

39. Be a Listening Post. AAM is proud to partner with the Nonprofit Listening Post Project, directed by the Center for Civil Society Studies at Johns Hopkins University. This nationwide project keeps a finger on the pulse of nonprofits through periodic surveys across the nonprofit sector, including many museums. By responding to periodic questionnaires, you help create meaningful data about the museum sector, thereby enhancing our field-wide advocacy tools. Visit www.jhu.edu/listeningpost for more information.

40. Link your website to www.speakupformuseums.org. By linking your museum's website to AAM's advocacy website, you can encourage your visitors and supporters to join in advocating for museums. Web stickers are available on www.speakupformuseums.org.

41. Engage your staff and volunteers. Add an advocacy update to staff meetings and volunteer meetings. Share information learned from AAM's Advocacy Alerts and discuss possible actions that can be taken.

42. Learn about the Congressional Record. This is a record of all statements and speeches made by all members of Congress. You can ask your members of Congress to submit a statement supporting one of your museum's achievements. You can also search for other information about your member of Congress. Members of Congress often acknowledge a museum's accreditation by placing a statement in the Congressional Record. You can learn more at www.congress.gov or see Chapter 9.

43. Follow your museum's profile in the news. By doing this, you can also get a sense of what your elected officials and other community leaders are reading about your museum. Visit the Google news website or a similar one, and set up free alerts for your museum's name so you know when it shows up in the press and how you are being covered. You can also follow how your elected officials are being covered in the media.

44. Profile legislators in your newsletter. You can highlight something they are working on, or ask them to write a guest column about a memorable experience visiting a museum. Be sure to send them a copy of the newsletter pointing out where they've been mentioned.

45. Be civic-minded. Offer to host a voter registration drive (contact the Board of Elections in your state for more information.) Or simply provide information about registering to vote on your museum's website or at the front desk. Voter information for every state can be found at www.speakup-formuseums.org.

46. Contact local school districts and offer to host regional history or science fairs.

47. Visit www.grants.gov to learn about federal grant opportunities. If you apply for a grant, ask your elected officials to write a letter of support. This could be both helpful to your application and strengthen your relationship with the elected official and his or her staff. (And if they write a letter of support, be sure to say thank you!)

48. Invite an elected official to speak at an upcoming meeting of your Board of Directors.

49. Tell Congress about the critical role museums play in education. AAM has a template letter on its advocacy website that can be personalized and sent electronically.

50. If your museum holds a major annual event (a Gala or Leadership Luncheon, for example), consider asking elected officials to serve as Honorary Co-Chairs.

51. Encourage your board of directors to complete an Advocacy Inventory during their next board meeting. See Chapter 3 for more information.

52. Create your museum's one-page economic impact statement and send it to your legislators. You can find this template on www.speakupfor museums.org and can send it automatically through the "Contact Congress" feature.

53. Provide this book to all of your board members and put advocacy on the agenda of the next board meeting.

54. Make a donation today! Your tax-deductible contribution helps AAM continue to advocate for museums on behalf of the whole field. You can donate directly toward advocacy for museums on www.speakupformuseums.org.

55. Create a media list. One way to get on the radar of an elected official is to get your museum covered in the local media. To create a media outreach list, consider which local publications cover issues related to your museum (arts, history, culture, science, etc.) Share news about new exhibits, public programs, and grants received.

56. Record audio/video testimonials. You can ask your staff, board of directors, or visitors to record their thoughts on why museums deserve public support or why they are essential. You can then share these with your elected officials, show them at a public event, or post them on your website.

57. Join AAM! AAM is committed to field-wide advocacy, and has identified advocacy as one of four goals in its strategic plan. By supporting your national association, you add your voice to our efforts that support museums of all types, sizes, and regions.

I bet that in reading through this list, you discovered some things you already do that you may not have thought of as "advocacy." If so, great!

If not, you now have many options for how you—and your volunteers, board of directors, staff, and supporters—can begin to advocate today.

And perhaps you even have some great advocacy ideas that didn't make it onto this list. If so, we want to hear from you. You can contact us through AAM's advocacy website at (yes, you guessed it) www.speakupformuseums.org.

And thanks.

"The only thing to do with good advice is pass it on. It is never any use to oneself."

– Oscar Wilde

Chapter 7

Expert Insider Advice from Elected and Public Officials

We've already covered a lot of ground, from how to get started to crafting just the right message. Now it is time to hear it straight from the experts, the insiders, the ones who, after all, we are trying to influence: elected and public officials.

The Honorable Jan Perry, Councilwoman, Los Angeles City Council, addressing advocates at the 2010 AAM Annual Meeting and MuseumExpo™ in Los Angeles in a session on advocacy:

"My deputy is a resource for me because she serves as an interface with museum staffs, with advocates, and people who are in the museum community, and keeps me abreast of new initiatives, new shows, what the demographic reach is on that show and how we can help fill the void. She is constantly developing our databases and our lists to make sure that we connect organizations and constituents with museum programs. That way, we are continuing to constantly build our relationships."

The Honorable Rush Holt, Congressman, New Jersey, addressing Museums Advocacy Day attendees in 2010:

"All of that will derive from the stories you tell…Do it by telling a story. Yes, legislation comes down to numbers and legalese, but it always begins with a story. That is the [most] effective lobbying."

The Honorable Mike Enzi, U.S. Senator, Wyoming, accepting a Congressional award during Museums Advocacy Day 2009:

"Sen. [Edward] Kennedy and I formed the Senate Cultural Caucus to place some emphasis on arts and museums and libraries. It's kind of an interesting working relationship because he is the 3rd most liberal senator and I'm the 4th most conservative senator, which shows that your work transcends everything."

The Honorable Carolyn Maloney, Congresswoman, New York, addressing Museums Advocacy Day attendees in 2010:

"Advocacy is a job for everyone and Advocacy Days are important. It is your chance to personally tell the story of why museums are important…We rely on our constituents to tell us what's important. We really do. It helps us really form our priorities. We rely on constituents to keep these issues on the front burner, and you make a tremendous difference."

The Honorable Todd Gloria, Councilman, San Diego City Council:

"As a former congressional aide, I believe the role [of staff] is incredibly important. As a current city councilmember, I know I depend on my staff to be in more places than I can, work on solving more constituent concerns than I could address personally, and provide me input and advice on policy matters. I work with my staff very closely and hope my constituents feel as comfortable with them.

"All information is welcome and appreciated, and I understand it is difficult for people and groups to know the best tools to use for each elected representative with whom they connect. For me, personal stories are always most impactful. Obviously, facts are critical, as well; personal accounts make facts more substantial and meaningful.

"Form letters are never as effective as individualized statements. I depend on public input to inform the decisions I make, but personalized stories and rationale for advocacy are absent when someone just clicks "send" or signs their name to a letter. When form letters are used, they are most effective when they come only from the district I represent.

"I am impressed when a person or group approaches me with a defined issue or problem, articulates how my district and constituents are impacted, and how it may be solved. Having purposeful dialogue adds significantly to these 'meet and greet' opportunities and provides me with a direct avenue to help."

The Honorable Aileen Adams, Los Angeles Deputy Mayor for Strategic Partnerships, addressing advocates in a session on advocacy at the 2010 AAM Annual Meeting and MuseumExpo:

"As someone who has served at all levels of government—as a Deputy Mayor for the city, a State Cabinet Member, and a Presidential Appointee in the U.S. Justice Department—I want to emphasize that, in my experience, government officials at all levels—city, state, and federal—are accessible to you. You just need to ask to meet with them in the right way. Here is a short ten-point plan of things you may want to keep in mind about accessing and interacting with public officials.

1. Be aggressive in setting up face-to-face meetings with public officials. Public officials are there to be accessible. Many public officials have an 'open door' policy. I don't think there is anyone who calls me, no matter how busy

I am, whose call I don't respond to. Never think that there is a barrier between your museum and a public official. The reason the public official is in their position is to serve you and to be accessible to you. Listening to the community and to their constituents is very much a part of their job.

2. Research public officials' backgrounds and interests. Before you set up a meeting, learn about a public official's history and passions. Know what their priorities are and what committees they serve on. Research what their connections are to culture and to museums. Try to link what you do to their interests. For example, if a legislator's primary interest is in education, you should be prepared to speak about the educational impact of your museum and the ways in which you partner with schools and enhance their curricula.

3. Get to know their staff. It is the staff who often brief public officials about important topics, help set their appointments, and write their talking points. A staff member can be an extremely important ally. If you go to a meeting expecting to talk with a public official and he or she doesn't show up, then take advantage of meeting with a top aide. Don't be disappointed, and always take time to befriend and educate a staff member, who can be a direct and powerful link to the public official.

4. Build a relationship. It should be a strategy of yours to build a relationship with public officials over time and to build it in every way that you can. For example, when you go to an event where a public official is speaking, ask a question. Go up to the official afterward and introduce yourself. Whenever you have an event, invite the public official and their staff to come and be introduced or say a few words.

5. Offer your museum as a meeting venue. Often public officials need venues to have community meetings to interact with their constituents. If it's possible, offer your museum as a place for the public official to have a dialogue with the community and emphasize its importance as a 'community space.' For example, the California Science Center in Los Angeles recently served as a location for a congressional hearing about all of the federal funding coming into Los Angeles and its impact.

6. Invite public officials to participate in press conferences and openings. When elected officials participate in press conferences, they become educated about your issues. In effect, they become your spokesperson. If you can include them in a press conference or an announcement of some kind, it will help to make them more knowledgeable about your issues.

7. Build a strong board that includes civic leaders. If you can, try to recruit to your board a couple of civic leaders who have access to public officials. They can help open political doors for you and facilitate discussions about public policy issues or needed legislation.

8. Remember there is power in numbers. Whenever you can, join with other museums to deliver a joint message or request to a public official. Public officials are very aware of the amount of mail that they receive on any given topic, so letter-writing campaigns can be effective.

9. Communicate effectively. It is extremely important to learn to deliver your message effectively and concisely. You have to put a human face on your work. You can't just be a statistic and talk about the number of visitors you have. To help a public official understand your impact, use vignettes about real people who have been impacted by your museum. You can produce inexpensively a short, 3- to 5-minute film about the power of your programs, and allow the public official to actually see the faces and hear the voices of the people impacted most by the services you provide. Your visitors can be your most effective spokespeople.

It's essential to be able to deliver your core message briefly and succinctly—in five minutes or less. Be able to describe your museum and what you need from the public official in a very concise and powerful way. Often you may think you have half an hour to talk with a public official, but because of his or her complicated schedule, you end up having to deliver your message walking down a hallway on the way to a vote. Practice your key points and be able to deliver your message quickly. Focus on one or two key issues. Have an 'ask.' Tell them specifically how they can help you. After the meeting, always write a thank-you note. People remember being thanked.

10. **Never underestimate the power of your economic message.** Many museums contribute to the economic well being of their communities in a number of ways. For example, some museums are essential in promoting cultural tourism. In Los Angeles, tourism is our greatest economic engine, generating over $12 billion a year. Twenty-five percent of these tourists are cultural tourists who come to our city primarily to visit a cultural venue—usually a museum. They spend 35% of all tourist dollars, generating thousands of jobs in hotels and restaurants and other sectors that cater to tourists. Many museums also create jobs through their construction programs, as well as the staff they hire.

"Of all of the above advice, I think the most difficult is figuring out exactly how to put 'a human face' on the extremely important work that you do. An example of this is a speech I recently heard by Paula Madison, who is a top executive at NBC Universal and serves as a Los Angeles City Library Commissioner. She told a large museum crowd recently about how she grew up in poverty in Harlem. She found refuge at New York's American Museum of Natural History, where she would go to learn, to explore, and to be inspired every day after school. She described the museum and its staff as her most important teachers, without whom she would not have been able to break through the barriers of poverty and become a leading executive. In effect, she put her own powerful human face on the important work of that museum—a vivid and memorable reminder of the extraordinary educational impact that they have on the lives of disadvantaged youth.

"It is up to those who work in museums to be key messengers and communicators to public officials about the unique and important roles museums play in so many areas as crucial educational assets and economic engines that deserve significant support from the public sector."

The Honorable [Dr.] Anne-Imelda Radice, former Director, Institute of Museum and Library Services, speaking in 2009 to Museums Advocacy Day participants:

"What I have learned in my visits [to Capitol Hill] is that although the members and the senators and the staff people are very delighted to see me and they always tell me that, they then say, 'But we'd rather see our constituents. Yes, Anne, you represent the administration. Yes, Anne, you represent a body of interest, but we need to hear from the people who actually voted for us and that is essential.'

"One of the reasons that the library folks have been so successful, I believe, is that they have been as a unit and now you are a unit. I can't begin to tell you the difference when I look out and see you all here…I think what's really important is that you all present a unified front about the value of culture and what culture does for your communities…

"You have compelling cases not only for the preservation of a cultural message or a collection, but you are additional learning for schools. You are a heart of the community and that makes a difference…You took the time to be here. Not just because this is a challenging time. There are always challenging times. This one is a little more difficult than others. You're here because you believe in what you do and you also believe in what everybody else does. That's powerful and I really, really recommend you keep that as a focus as you go up to [Capitol] Hill."

The Honorable Maxine Waters, Congresswoman, California, addressing Museums Advocacy Day attendees in 2010:

"I was pleased to see that this day is named Museums Advocacy Day, because that is exactly what you have to do: advocate, especially given the economic climate in this country. You are going to have to be real advocates for museums. You are going to have to spend some time with legislators educating about the importance of museums and the relationship of museums to education and all that we try to do as we invest in our young people to help them to become the adults that they can become. As you know, when we are in economic difficulty, when the states are in economic crisis, the first thing they want to cut? The museums. And they will tell you everything else is more important and they've got to fund health and education and welfare, and all of that. And I know that you know how to do it, but you must be able to articulate that none of that works without the museums. It is the connecting glue, to the degree that they are trying to educate young people about all of these issues. If they have an opportunity to visit the museums, and to have interaction with the kind of exhibits that you have, then they can learn better. That their minds can be opened up, and that art and culture is important to a civilized nation. I know you know how to do it, but I just want to tell you here this morning that you've got to be a little aggressive in doing it. Don't be too nice. Because if you're too nice, you're going to be left. And in this very competitive era that we are in, you're going to have to remind all these legislators how important it is to point out these wonderful institutions and venues in their communities."

The Honorable Betty McCollum, Congresswoman, Minnesota, addressing Museums Advocacy Day attendees in 2009:

"So when you're here talking to your member of Congress don't be shy about probing them. What was it like the first time you went into a museum? Do your students have access to moving collections and exhibits in the district? What can I do for you back home to make this connectivity even more real for you? So don't be afraid to ask questions and to offer help. And then after you're done meeting with the folks here in Washington, I'm going to encourage each and every one of you to do something [else]. And that is to go to the district office. Get to know the district director. Invite the district staff out to see what's going on, because lots of times the member of Congress isn't going to be able make it, but the district director's talking to the chief of staff, talking to the member."

The Honorable Marcia Fudge, Congresswoman, Ohio, addressing Museums Advocacy Day attendees in 2009:

"If young people and all people who believe that history is important don't have institutions like museums, we are lost…And I want you to continue to be the place where young people can come and learn. I grew up in a place where we didn't hear things about museums or theaters. My teachers are the ones who first took me to a museum, to a theater. And from there the love of learning that I had then and that I have now was nurtured. It was encouraged. I saw things that I had only dreamed up in my head. And then I saw things that I could never have even dreamed of. So I hope that you will continue to let young people and the people of this country understand how important the arts are, understand how important history is, and as well to let them know what a major force museums and the arts industry can be in any community, because even when people don't have money they will go to a theater. They will come to a museum. In times like these it is very, very important that you are there, and I thank you so much for your work."

The Honorable John Lewis, Congressman, Georgia, and civil rights icon, who delivered the keynote address to Museums Advocacy Day participants in 2009:

"As museum administrators you have an obligation, a mission and a mandate to do what you can to use your nonprofit tax exemption, and we want to help you use the tax code to make your work easier but also to be enlightening and inspiring. You know we can build bridges and we need bridges. We can build highways and we need highways. But I don't think people are going to be inspired by our bridges, by our highways, our roads. But what we place in these places of history reflects our true selves, that we inspire people for generations yet unborn. It's one thing to live in America and travel to some other part of the world, places like India, and see simple places where Gandhi spent the night, where he fasted, where he went out near a river, and see a marker. Do what you can to make life of yesteryear today real for all of our people, so we all can be inspired to get in the way, to stand up, to say no or to say yes. You can do it. You must do it."

The Honorable Kate Segal, State Representative, Michigan (former Congressional staffer and currently Michigan House Democratic Floor Leader)

"The most effective groups take the time to build a relationship. Don't come in during a crisis and expect immediate action, especially if we've never previously had a chance to discuss your issue. It's better if you have developed a relationship with us, and we have a good understanding of your issues and the work you do, before you need our help.

"It's important to show your impact on the community. For a museum, you might bring along residents of the community who have been impacted by your programs. And how has the program helped children in your community? That's a really effective message.

"I had a group of low-income parents come visit me to discuss how their kids with special needs were faring in the local schools. I know it took a lot of effort for the advocates to arrange such a meeting, and I know that this group of parents had previously had very limited interaction with government officials, but it made a huge impact to hear their stories directly.

"If I represent you in Lansing, I want to know what you do, what you think, and I want to know who you are so I can seek you out on relevant issues. I really pay attention to letters when they come from my constituents. At my weekly staff meetings, I always get a report on who has been in touch with my office and on which issues. We keep track of it, and we respond to every constituent, so it does make a difference when you contact us.

"Advocates should also be careful in the language they use. Don't be threatening. If you say something like, 'I voted for you and…' that's probably not going to go over so well.

"Take the time to personally thank people after they voted or took action, especially when it was on a difficult issue. If you are going to take the time to be an advocate, you should really also take the time to say thank you. And if you can send a personal note, that makes a big impression. You know, use a stamp. You'd be surprised how few people send personal, handwritten thank-you notes, so yours will really stand out and be remembered.

"Treat staff as if they were gold. You may sometimes feel like you are being put off by staff. However, if you treat them well they could be your biggest advocates in getting your issue in front of me. They have a very hard job and you have to remember they are juggling so many things. If you treat staff poorly, your issue could end up at the bottom of the pile. I still remember some of the people who were unkind or impatient with me when I served as a Scheduler on Capitol Hill many years ago. Then as I became a Legislative Assistant and then Senior Legislative Assistant, I still remembered.

"My best advice for advocates is this: Don't take no for an answer. Don't take 'I'll look into it' for an answer. I find some of my colleagues never commit to anything and they are never held accountable for it. It drives me nuts! If you ask a direct question, you deserve a direct answer, and you shouldn't let people be slippery about things. You might hear, 'Great to see you. You know I love museums. Thanks for coming by.' Don't let them get away with that. Sometimes you'll have to ask more than once, and in more than one way, but don't let them get away with the non-committal answer."

The Honorable Jeff Waldstreicher, Maryland State Delegate

"Advocacy groups are always at their best when they bring constituents to a meeting. As much as I love my job—and I'm thankful for the privilege every day—the work of a legislator can occasionally be exhausting and monotonous. So I'm thankful whenever I can make a personal connection with a constituent, such as a shared hometown or house of worship. When advocacy groups can facilitate that personal connection, they're two steps ahead of those that cannot."

"I encourage citizens to utilize and support their local museums, which serve as a wonderful resource for communities. There is great value for citizens in the arts, historic collections and museums. They are a reflection of our culture and people, and are important to our history and national identity. Children and young learners benefit tremendously from art programs in the schools. These activities make for well-rounded citizens, tomorrow's leaders. Museums play an important role in our lives."

– Sen. Tom Coburn (R-OK)

Chapter 8

What Did He Just Say? Decoding Congress-Speak

Say what?

You may be surprised that the quote above comes from Senator Tom Coburn, who has offered numerous amendments to restrict or eliminate funding for museums. How can this be?

The truth is that he really does think highly of museums. He is reportedly a big fan of opera, too (his daughter is an acclaimed opera singer). In 2010, Senator Coburn supported the reauthorization of the Institute of Museum and Library Services, which he is on record describing as an accountable, well-run agency with a peer-reviewed grant-making process.

His issue? He is extremely concerned about the national debt and the persistent federal budget deficit. And he has a particular issue with anything that is considered an earmark.

It can be tricky to navigate this kind of thing.

Here's another example. Many times, following Museums Advocacy Day, participants report back that their members of Congress just love museums, and that they will definitely support our issues! When we follow up, we find that they didn't want to say no, but did not actually agree to support the specific request.

That's why it's important to know exactly what you are asking for, and then to follow up at the appropriate time to make sure you get a specific answer. (Even if you don't get the answer you wanted, as a constituent, you certainly deserve an answer!)

When you contact a member of Congress, you will frequently get a "form letter" response. It often looks something like this:

Dear Constituent,

Thank you so much for contacting me about the Basic Issue Act, introduced by Rep. Jones on such-and-such date. It's always great to hear from constituents like you.

As you know, this bill will do this basic thing, that basic thing, and that other basic thing. It is currently being considered by the House Subcommittee on Really Basic Stuff.

I recognize the importance of this issue, because basic facts are what we need to make good decisions, and I am aware that basic facts can be hard to come by, especially in this difficult economy. Please be assured that I will keep your views in mind as Congress considers this issue.

Does this sound familiar?

You may have received a similar letter if you have ever contacted members of Congress. And to be fair, it's still good to know that your issue is at least on their radar screen. Chances are, if the issue does come up, they will revisit your letter at that time, and may even reach out to you for additional information. The correspondence systems are designed to do just that.

But how do you get a real answer? That's the question.

First, keep in mind that members of Congress often don't want to commit to a position on something unless—and until—they really have to. That's why the relationship building is so important. And that's why you have to be persistent.

Think about it: members of Congress certainly don't want to disappoint you. You are, after all, kind of their boss. Your community elected them, and can un-elect them, too.

You may already deal with this in your own life. Say one of your colleagues stops by with an idea. While you appreciate his or her good intentions, you just don't think the idea will fly. But you don't want to hurt your colleague's feelings, so you say, "Wow, let me think about that. It's an interesting idea. I'll get back to you. How's that other project you are working on coming along?"

You know who you are.

In this case, in order to get more specific feedback from you, perhaps your colleague could schedule a meeting to discuss the idea in further detail. If he or she is a good advocate (and remember, advocacy is defined as anytime you are making your case), he or she will bring facts, figures, a compelling story, and a very clear "ask": What do you think of this idea? Can you think of any potential opposition? What information might we need in order to make a decision on this? Who else needs to be involved? How shall I proceed from here?

Wouldn't it be a little harder to say no to this person?

Members of Congress manage people and issues the same way. They may even employ a lot of technical details in an effort to give you an answer, without taking a position. Sometimes a member of Congress will (perhaps inadvertently) try to confuse you. You might hear this:

Dear Constituent,

Thank you so much for contacting me about the Basic Issue Technical Amendments Act, which would amend the Basic Issues Act of 1994 to call for a minimum fiduciary requirement for all tax exempt institutions that proffer funding requests exceeding $100 million in discretionary spending. The bill was dropped on such-and-such date and has been referred to the House Committee on Commerce, the Ways and Means Committee, and the Financial Services Committee. As it has multiple referrals, it could take a while for it to be considered, unless there is not a quorum or the committee tables the motion to consider the bill.

I care deeply about this issue and will plan to ask unanimous consent to move the previous question on the amendment to instruct the House. If we are unable to get the bill out of the committee, I will draft a discharge petition to bring this to the House Floor.

Okay, that may be a bit of an exaggeration.

But the basic tenet holds true: you sometimes have to sort through a lot of gobbledygook.

Don't be intimidated. In fact, if you get an answer that you don't understand, use this as an opportunity to write again and ask for clarification. You know what they say about the squeaky wheel.

To help avoid confusion, before you contact an office, be sure you know exactly what you are asking for, and make your request very clear.

For example, you might be asking elected officials to:

- **Introduce a bill,** which means you want them to initiate, sponsor, or otherwise spearhead a legislative effort.
- **Cosponsor (sign on to) a bill,** which means you want them to formally support a bill introduced by another member of Congress.
- **Sign on to a "Dear Colleague" letter,** which means you want them to add their name to a letter circulated by another member of Congress, often in support of a funding request.
- **Offer an amendment,** which means you want them to spearhead an addition, deletion, or substitution in pending legislation, either in committee or on the House or Senate Floor.

- **Support an amendment,** which means you want them to vote in favor of another member of Congress's amendment, or make a public statement on its behalf (either in committee or on the House or Senate Floor).

- **Oppose an amendment,** which means you want them to vote against another member of Congress' amendment, or make a public statement against it (either in committee or on the House or Senate Floor).

- **Vote yes or no,** which means you want them to cast a vote for or against a measure, either in committee or on the House or Senate Floor.

- **Make an inquiry,** which means you want them to ask a federal agency or other (usually federal) entity about a situation, either by writing a letter or making a phone call to the entity.

- **Make a public statement,** which means you want them to go on record about an issue: in the media, on the House or Senate floor, in committee, in the Congressional Record, or elsewhere.

- **Hold a hearing,** which means you want them to urge a committee to take up an issue, either on Capitol Hill or in a field hearing. If they happen to chair a committee or subcommittee that has jurisdiction, they might be able to call for such a hearing directly.

- **Be aware of the impact of legislation on museums,** which means that while there is not a specific legislative ask at this time, you want them to know you are in fact a stakeholder in this issue.

In most cases, they either did or didn't. Either they will or they won't. There really isn't much wiggle room. If they decide to take no action, they should have to explain why. Constituents like you deserve to know why.

That's why your ask must be crystal clear, and you must be persistent, so they can't give you an excuse about not having been aware of your issue. It's true they have a lot on their plates, but if you are persistent in your advocacy, you will keep your issue on their radar screen and they will be more likely to take action.

They might tell you, "The bill has been referred to the Commerce Committee." But they could probably still cosponsor the bill.

They might tell you, "I'm not on that Committee." But they could still contact that committee and ask that the bill be taken up.

They might tell you, "This is a Senate bill, and hasn't yet come before the House." But they could still investigate whether there will be a House version and, if not, consider introducing it themselves.

See how that works?

They might tell you, "The House has not yet taken up that bill." But they could still contact the sponsor to see how they might help to move the bill. For example, there could be someone in a position of leadership who is blocking the bill, and your elected official can approach him or her directly. And that is the ultimate goal: to turn your members of Congress into advocates for your cause!

The good news is that you don't have to sort through all of this on your own. AAM's advocacy website www.speakupformuseums.org has provided template letters on a variety of topics with a built-in ask that is clear and concise. These letters can be personalized and sent electronically with just a few clicks. And we are constantly updating the letters to ensure that your electronic communications through the website are complete, concise, and clear.

You'll also find information about how federal issues affect museums, who represents you in Congress, what committees they are on, who their key staff members are, and news about AAM's latest advocacy efforts. You can also find information about those who represent you at the state level.

You're welcome!

Here's a final thought for you: After a while, you won't have to sort through all the gobbledygook anymore because you will have begun a dialogue—and then a relationship—that will extend beyond your correspondence over the official email systems. You will be able to rely on elected officials and their staffs for straight answers, and they will rely on you for your expertise and advice. And chances are, as you deepen the relationship, they will have a harder time saying no, especially because they will come to know you as an empowered, impassioned, knowledgeable, savvy advocate—and expert—on the many ways that museums are essential to our communities.

"Information is the currency of democracy."

– Thomas Jefferson

Chapter 9

Additional Resources and Burning Questions

Let me save you a lot of time right off the bat.

One of the most useful websites to help you advocate for museums is the American Association of Museums' advocacy website, www.speakupfor museums.org

On www.speakupformuseums.org, you can:

- Identify your federal and state legislators and their office and key staff information
- Personalize and send (electronically or via postal mail) letters to your members of Congress on a variety of issues (templates provided)
- Find the latest facts and figures about museums
- Sign up to receive Advocacy Alerts and Legislative Updates
- See recent and past Advocacy Alerts
- Learn about Museums Advocacy Day activities
- See video clips from Museums Advocacy Day events (including testimonials from members of Congress about the value of museums!)

- Register for AAM's Online Advocacy Trainings and access archived training materials and recordings
- Complete a quick and easy Economic Impact Statement for your museum and share it with your legislators
- Find Issue Briefs on federal legislative issues affecting museums
- Follow AAM's activities with Congress and federal agencies
- Find information about recent congressional hearings and activity affecting museums, including congressional footage and statements by members of Congress
- Review letters and statements by AAM President Ford W. Bell and AAM on key issues
- Learn about Congress and key committees whose work affects museums
- Access nationwide voter information, including your polling place and state voter information
- Find web stickers to link your museum's website to the Speak Up for Museums Contact Congress and Voter Information features
- Find complete contact information for AAM's Government Relations Office

(And now you know why we refer to it so many times in this book!)

One of the best places to learn about museums is the **American Association of Museums Information Center**. The Information Center provides resources to help museum professionals succeed in their careers and help museums achieve field-wide standards and apply best practices. All individual members of AAM have access to the extensive library of Online Resources that have been individually reviewed, categorized, and described for their usefulness to museum professionals. Here you can find detailed information about:

- Collections Stewardship
- Education & Interpretation
- Case Statements
- Federal Government Funding Opportunities
- Grant-writing
- Accountability & Ethics
- Community Engagement
- Marketing & Public Relations
- And more!

Museum members at the institutional level have additional access to a wide variety of sample documents from accredited museums, plus customized reference services from Information Center staff. For more information on this free service for AAM members visit www.aam-us.org/infocenter.

Now that you know about the information available on AAM's website, we thought it would be helpful to answer some of the questions we frequently are asked. Much of this chapter is related to Capitol Hill, but some of this information may be similar to how things work in your state or local government.

What is the difference between a member of Congress and a representative or senator?

All members of the U.S. House and U.S. Senate are referred to as members of Congress. House members are commonly called representatives (or congressman/congresswoman) and Senate members are commonly called senators.

At the federal level, each of us is represented by one U.S. Representative (who usually represents a portion of the state, or "Congressional district") and two U.S. Senators (who each represent the entire state). The average size of a Congressional district is 650,000 people.

How can I keep track of who will be up for election in any given year?

All members of the U.S. House are up for re-election every two years. U.S. Senators serve a six-year term, and one-third of them are up for re-election every two years. Mid-term elections refer to the election years between presidential elections. The website www.vote411.org, run by the League of Women Voters Education Fund, provides up-to-date information on elections and candidates.

What does it mean when there is a "new Congress"?

Every two years marks the beginning of a new Congressional session, denoted by a number. The First Congress convened on March 4, 1789. In 2011, the 112th Congress convened. In 2013, the 113th Congress will convene.

In each new Congress, all previously pending bills and resolutions must be re-introduced in order to be considered. New members of Congress, who replaced members who retired or lost their re-election bids, will be sworn in. Leadership elections will often take place at the beginning of a new Congress.

Who's in charge in Congress?

In the House, the party in power (or "majority") elects a Speaker of the House, a Majority Leader, and a Majority Whip. The minority party elects a Minority Leader and a Minority Whip. The Whip's job is to "count votes" by keeping track of how members of their party will vote on a variety of key issues. There may also be a Chief Deputy Whip and several additional Deputy Whips.

In the Senate, the party in power elects a Majority Leader and a Majority Whip. The minority party elects a Minority Leader and a Minority Whip. The Vice President of the United States actually serves as the ex-officio President of the Senate, but as a rule does not preside over the proceedings or vote, unless it is to break a tie vote. The President Pro Tempore is the presiding officer of the Senate and is usually the most senior member of the majority party.

Parties may also establish additional leadership positions, and you can find out who's currently in charge by visiting www.house.gov and www.senate.gov. The following groups also elect or select leaders:

The House Republican Conference (www.gop.gov) is made up of all Republicans in the House. The House Democratic Caucus (www.dems.gov) is made up of all Democrats in the House. Each group typically elects a Chair, Vice Chair, and Secretary.

House Republicans also have a House Republican Steering Committee and a House Republican Policy Committee. A "Steering" Committee determines committee assignments for other members of its party. A "Policy" Committee advises the leadership on policy issues. House Democrats have combined these functions into one committee, the House Democratic Steering and Policy Committee.

The Senate Republican Conference (http://republican.senate.gov) is made up of all Republicans in the Senate, and its policy arm is the Senate Republican Policy Committee (http://rpc.senate.gov). The Senate Democratic Conference (http://democrats.senate.gov) is made up of all Democrats in the Senate and its policy arm is the Senate Democratic Policy Committee (http://dpc.senate.gov).

What is a Congressional Caucus?

A caucus is an informal group of members of Congress who share an interest in certain policy issues, such as the Senate Cultural Caucus, the Congressional Hispanic Caucus, or the Congressional Caucus on Missing and Exploited Children. A caucus may hold briefings, spearhead a legislative effort, circulate information to other members of Congress, or otherwise champion its issue in Congress.

There are more than two hundred caucuses in Congress, and members of Congress may choose to join as many as they wish. They frequently point to their membership in a caucus as evidence of their commitment to an issue. You may have heard your member of Congress mention belonging to the Congressional Arts Caucus, the Congressional Humanities Caucus, the Congressional Historic Preservation Caucus, or the Congressional Life Sciences Caucus.

What about a Congressional Museums Caucus?

I agree that we need one! And while there hasn't been one to date, we at AAM are interested in this idea. What would it take? Ideally, we would work with advocates and colleagues in the field to identify a (preferably) bipartisan pair of members of Congress to decide to initiate and co-chair the Caucus. Their staffs would then register the Caucus with the House Clerk's office and encourage other members of Congress to join. (This would most likely happen in the House of Representatives because in the Senate, there is already the Senate Cultural Caucus.) Our job as advocates would be to urge our U.S. Representatives to join the Caucus, and then work closely with the Co-Chairs and their staffs to find ways for them to highlight the value of museums to their colleagues in Congress and champion issues that would help support museums. Having a Congressional Caucus certainly wouldn't take the place of having a strong grassroots base of museum advocates, but it would be very helpful for advancing our agenda in Congress. Perhaps a future edition of this book will report that a Congressional Museums Caucus has been established. Stay tuned!

How do committees operate, and why are they so important?

Most bills that are considered by Congress go through at least one committee, where much of the substantive work on the bill is done. Committees also hold hearings, investigations, and markups (where they literally "mark up" the bill with additions, deletions, or other changes). Some committees also hold field hearings.

Members of Congress are each assigned to one or more committees, and each committee is given jurisdiction over a specific set of issues and federal agencies (usually you can find this on the committee websites).

A few committees are more involved in issues related to museums, such as the Appropriations Committee (which determines funding levels for various programs and federal agencies), the committees that oversee education, and the committees that oversee tax policy (and just to confuse things, they have different names in the House and Senate).

To make it easy to navigate, here are the key committees and their website addresses:

- House Committee on Appropriations: http://appropriations.house.gov/
- House Education and the Workforce Committee*: http://edworkforce. house.gov/
- House Ways and Means Committee: http://waysandmeans.house.gov/
- Senate Committee on Appropriations: http://appropriations.senate.gov/
- Senate Committee on Health, Education, Labor, and Pensions (also known as "the HELP Committee"): http://help.senate.gov/
- Senate Finance Committee: http://finance.senate.gov/

*sometimes named the House Education and Labor Committee, depending on which party is in charge. The above name is correct at press time.

There are other committees that can be relevant to museums (the House Science Committee or the Senate Committee on Indian Affairs, for example), but the above six are considered the key committees for most issues affecting museums.

Each committee also has a Chair (generally the most senior member of the committee from the majority party), a Ranking Member (generally the most senior member of the committee from the minority party), and usually several subcommittees. Each subcommittee also has a Chair and a Ranking Member. It is important to work with both sides of the aisle (Republican and Democrat) to ensure the widest possible support for your issue.

When the House and Senate pass different versions of a bill that need to be reconciled, a Conference Committee (comprised of both House and Senate members) is formed to sort out the differences. Finally, there are a few committees that include members of both the House and Senate, but do not pass legislation; these are called Joint Committees and they typically study issues, hold hearings, and release reports.

You can learn more about House and Senate Committees by visiting www.house.gov and www.senate.gov.

What is the difference between a bill, a resolution, an Act, and a law?

A bill is a legislative proposal. Each bill is assigned a number once it is formally introduced (or "dropped" as in "dropped into the hopper," which refers to the box that new bills are physically dropped into). In Congress, "H.R." denotes bills that originate in the House of Representatives and "S." denotes bills that originate in the Senate. A bill becomes a law when it is passed by both the House and the Senate and signed by the president.

A resolution is a type of legislation used as a way for members of Congress to publicly express their collective position on a situation or event (for example, expressing sympathy over an international tragedy or congratulations to a championship college team). It does not have the force of law. A resolution is designated by "H. Res." or "S. Res." when it expresses the view of the House or Senate. Similarly, a "Concurrent Resolution" (designated by "H.Con.Res." or "S.Con.Res.") is introduced to express the sentiments of the Congress and is then considered by both the House and the Senate. A "Joint Resolution" (designated by "H.J.Res." or "S.J.Res.") is yet another type of resolution, and is usually reserved for Constitutional amendments.

An "Act" may refer either to a bill when it is introduced or to a law that has been enacted. For example, when the Family and Medical Leave Act of 1993 was first introduced, it was a legislative proposal. Today, the Family and Medical Leave Act is the law of the land.

What does it mean when a member of Congress sponsors or co-sponsors a bill?

When a bill or resolution gets introduced, it is usually spearheaded by one person, the sponsor. There may also be "original co-sponsors" who jointly introduce a bill, but there is still just one primary sponsor. In some cases, a bill will come to be known—formally or informally—by the name of the specific legislator(s) who introduced and moved the bill forward, e.g., the Bipartisan Campaign Reform Act of 2002, which came to be known as "McCain-Feingold" (after Senators John McCain of Arizona and Russ Feingold of Wisconsin) or the Sarbanes-Oxley Act of 2002, after Senator Paul Sarbanes of Maryland and Representative Mike Oxley of Ohio. Similarly, a provision of a bill will sometimes be named after the key supporter of that provision, such as Roth IRAs (named after Sen. William Roth of Delaware), or Pell grants (named after Sen. Claiborne Pell of Rhode Island).

Advocates often encourage members of Congress to co-sponsor legislation, which entails their staff contacting the primary sponsor's staff and saying, "Would you please add my boss's name to such-and-such bill? He/She would like to be a co-sponsor."

Any member of the House can co-sponsor House bills, and anyone in the Senate can co-sponsor Senate bills. There is no limit as to how many bills they can support at any given time. In the House, a member can become a co-sponsor of a bill at any point up to the time the committee passes the bill. In the Senate, a member can become a co-sponsor of a bill anytime before the vote takes place on the bill.

It is not necessary for a bill to have co-sponsors, but the number of co-sponsors is a good measure of how much support the bill has. Sometimes, members of Congress are told by the House or Senate leadership that their bill needs to have a certain number of co-sponsors before it will be considered for a vote.

The bottom line is this: urging your members of Congress to co-sponsor legislation is a very important part of the process. It is the first step toward getting your bill the attention it needs.

Who decides which bills get taken up?

Usually, the House or Senate majority leadership will decide which bills will be considered on the House or Senate floor. They consider the work of committees, the public support for a bill, their political agenda, and a host of other factors.

Who decides the various procedures by which bills are considered?

When a bill is considered, a procedure will be laid out for how the bill will be debated and voted upon. In the House, the bill will often go through the Rules Committee, which has the authority to determine whether any amendments—and which ones—will be considered. The Rules Committee may declare an "Open Rule," which means any germane (relevant) amendments can be considered. The House may also consider a bill under "Suspension of the Rules," where debate is limited, no amendments are allowed, and a vote by two thirds of those present is required for passage. This is usually reserved for non-controversial bills.

Much of the work of the Senate is done by Unanimous Consent (or "U.C."). This phrase is uttered very frequently and loosely translates to "Hey, if it's okay with everybody," as in, "I ask unanimous consent to revise and extend my remarks." When this phrase is used in relation to the consideration of a bill, it is usually a reflection of the fact that a) the bill is non-controversial and b) the leadership and relevant committee members have agreed to swift consideration (i.e., limited or no amendments), and therefore do not want to take up time on the Senate floor with a more exhaustive process. Any Senator can object to unanimous consent, and might do so to slow down (or block) a bill from moving forward.

Why is 60 considered a magic number in the Senate?

The Senate has 100 members (two from each state), so you would think that it would take just 51 votes to pass a bill. But not in the U.S. Senate. In the Senate, it pretty much takes the vote of 60 Senators to proceed on any measure. Here's why: In order to prevent a bill from being considered, a Senator may "filibuster," or use delaying tactics. These tactics may include extensive debate, offering procedural motions, or other actions, and may go on for many hours. The only way to end the delaying tactics is to invoke "cloture," which requires a super-majority vote of 60 Senators.

What is an amendment?

An amendment is a proposal to add, delete, or substitute the language of a bill. It can be offered when a Committee is considering a bill, or when the bill reaches the House or Senate floor. Sometimes amendments are offered in an attempt to undermine the original intent of (or "kill") the bill. This is often referred to as a "poison pill" amendment. In the House of Representatives, a bill may be subject to a "Rule" produced by the Rules Committee, which determines the manner in which a bill will be considered, including which amendments it will allow to be offered.

What is report language?

When a committee completes work on a bill, it usually creates a report that explains in detail the history, intent, and substance of a bill. The report may also set forth reporting requirements, spending instructions, or other directives to federal agencies. At times, an advocate may request that specific language be included in the report, because getting favorable report language can be another way to influence legislation, and it is a whole lot easier than getting actual bill language passed.

What's the deal with all the different types of votes in Congress?

At any given time, members of Congress may vote on a bill, vote on an amendment, vote to invoke cloture (or end a filibuster, which is a Senate maneuver used to block passage of legislation), vote on a quorum call (to determine if enough members of Congress are present to consider certain legislation), or vote to override a president's veto (which requires a two-thirds vote by those present in both the House and Senate). Sometimes there will be a simple roll call vote (which records the yeas and nays), and sometimes there will be a "voice vote," which does not involve recording how each member of Congress voted. Similarly, a member of Congress can ask for "Unanimous Consent" to proceed on—or agree to—a measure without a recorded vote.

What is the federal budget process and how is it related to the appropriations process?

Each year, the president proposes a federal budget to Congress, usually during the first week of February, for the next fiscal year beginning on October 1. The president's budget proposal establishes the priorities that the president will pursue that year, and more importantly, is a starting point for the many debates—on the budget and on appropriations—that will take place in Congress that year.

Then Congress usually passes a budget resolution, establishing its own set of priorities on both federal spending and taxation.

The president's budget and the Congressional budget may or may not be in alignment, but it doesn't matter much. Neither has any force of law.

Then the real work begins.

The real (more tangible) game in Congress is the annual appropriations process, by which a series of Appropriations subcommittees writes the bills that determine the exact amount of funding that each federal agency and program will be allotted in the following fiscal year.

The House and Senate each have an Appropriations Committee, and each currently has twelve subcommittees. Once a subcommittee passes its respective bill, it goes to the full Appropriations Committee, then to the House or Senate floor. Once passed by each chamber, the differences are reconciled in a House-Senate Conference Committee, and both chambers must again vote on the final version. Because of its enormous power to influence so much of what the federal government does, the Appropriations Committee is considered by many to be the most influential and powerful committee in Congress.

So when we ask for a certain funding level for the IMLS Office of Museum Services, we request it from both the House and Senate Appropriations Subcommittees on Health, Education, Labor, and Related Agencies (IMLS is considered an agency related to the U.S. Departments of Health and Human Services, Education, and Labor). Funding for the National Endowment for the Arts and the National Endowment for the Humanities is determined by the Appropriations Subcommittee on Interior, Environment and Related Agencies. Funding for the National Science Foundation comes from yet another subcommittee. And so on.

The process seems to go on all year. And it often does.

Sometimes Congress completes its work by the start of the new fiscal year (October 1), but more often it does not. In that case, to keep the government from shutting down, they must pass a Continuing Resolution (or "CR"), which usually keeps the government operating at current spending levels for a specific amount of time—days, weeks, or months.

Sometimes Congress will consider additional appropriations bills through-out the year. These are called supplemental appropriations, and are often in response to an emergency, a disaster, or a war. The 2009 economic stimulus bill (the American Recovery and Reinvestment Act) is a good example of this.

Sometimes Congress will consider a rescissions bill to cancel, or rescind, previously approved funds from being spent by federal agencies. Advocates are often concerned about a rescissions bill because it can put a hard-fought victory—an agency's increased funds, for example—back on the table for further negotiation. Imagine how you would feel if your museum's budget was partially rescinded partway through the year. It's not a pleasant process, but it can happen.

It should be noted that in some states, the terminology is completely reversed, so the "budget process" at the state level is actually more of a pro-cess to appropriate funds, i.e., an appropriations process.

Are you still with us?

If you are still wondering about the difference between the budget process and the appropriations process, here is an easy way to think about it:

The federal budget process is similar to how you might establish your museum's annual budget. You determine priorities, consider your operating costs, make estimations about your revenue and contributions, and then the year begins and you hope things go as planned!

Appropriations are more like a series of checkbooks or debit cards and rules for how money may be spent. Once passed, appropriations bills have the force of law.

What is an authorization?

When a federal agency or program is created by Congress, certain rules are set forth that outline what the agency is allowed to do, how the program will work, who will oversee the program, how the agency can spend money, etc. Sometimes the law names a specific amount of authorized funding, or it may just authorize "such sums as may be necessary" to carry out the program or agency. Either way, it is important to note that an authorization does not guarantee funding—it is more of a recommendation on the amount that should be provided. The actual funding is determined through the annual appropriations process, described above.

Many laws also include a provision requiring the program or agency to be reviewed every few years. This process is called re-authorization. In the case of IMLS, for example, the agency is due to be re-authorized every five years.

Sometimes a reauthorization occurs on time, but often it does not. An agency's authorization will then technically expire, but as long as they are allotted funding through the annual appropriations process, the agency and its programs will continue to exist.

It is common for agencies to go without being "authorized" for long periods. However, it is considered helpful to have the agency officially "authorized" as it competes for funding, especially in a challenging political and budgetary climate. Here's how:

Let's say a federal agency is *authorized* to receive $100 million each year, but during the appropriations process is only being *funded* at $50 million. You could make the case that the authorizing committee identified a critical unmet need and authorized the $100 million to address it. And you could make the case that Congress must act immediately to fully fund the agency. It still won't guarantee increased funding, but it could be a helpful argument in the appropriations process.

Do form letters, phone calls, and emails really make a difference?

This is a very common question and the answer is yes, but don't take my word for it. This has actually been studied in depth. The Partnership for a More Perfect Union (http://pmpu.org) conducts anonymous surveys with Congressional offices to determine what kind of communication by advocates is most effective. The last study was done in late 2010 and here is what they found.

Most staff (90%) agreed—and more than 60% strongly agreed—that responding to constituent communications is a high priority in their offices. The study showed that postal mail (90%) and email (88%) influenced an undecided member of Congress.

So what are the most effective strategies?

Good news: The Partnership for a More Perfect Union asked Congressional offices this question, too! Constituent visits to the Washington office (97%) and to the district/state office (94%) have "some" or "a lot" of influence on an undecided member of Congress, more than any other influence group or strategy. When asked about strategies directed to their offices back home, staffers said questions at town hall meetings (87%) and letters to the editor (80%) have "some" or "a lot" of influence. Nearly two-thirds of staff surveyed (64%) think Facebook is an important way to understand constituents' views, and nearly three-quarters (74%) think it is important for communicating their member's views.

If that doesn't convince you to get more involved with your elected officials, I don't know what will! It also makes a great case for participating in Museums Advocacy Day.

What exactly is an "Advocacy Day"?

An advocacy day is an opportunity for a particular field or industry to make a unified case to elected officials—either at the state or local level or to

Congress—on a set of issues of importance to the field. Museums Advocacy Day began in 2009 as a field-wide event, where museum staff, volunteers, trustees, students, and supporters gathered in Washington, DC, to make a coordinated case to Congress in support of museums.

Most industries hold an annual advocacy day and have been doing so for years—the dentists, the credit unions, the funeral directors, for example, all hold an advocacy day each year in Washington. Even the sand, gravel, and concrete industry holds an annual advocacy day. The good news is that now museums do, too!

Who's involved with Museums Advocacy Day, and who's invited?

The entire museum field is encouraged to participate in the two-day event on Capitol Hill. A Planning Committee, comprised of representatives from national, regional, and state museum associations and other supporters, ensures field-wide participation and input on a variety of issues related to the event.

I want to come to Museums Advocacy Day, but it's all pretty intimidating. How will I know what to say to my legislators?

First, you should know that AAM arranges all Capitol Hill appointments and provides an individual schedule for each participant. By the time you finish the day of advocacy and issues training, you will be ready—and excited about—your visits to Capitol Hill. Often you will be accompanied on your congressional visits by other advocates from your state and/or congressional district, so you can all make the case together! The ideal scenario is to bring a board member or two with you to Washington, so you can advocate for museums as a group.

And perhaps more important, policymakers—at the federal, state and local levels—know that they can't do their jobs without hearing from you. You have the expertise, perspective, and community impact that they need to know about. Your passion and your experience will speak volumes as you visit with elected officials.

How will I find my way around the Capitol complex? How does everything work?

The "mystique" about our nation's capital is really overblown. Getting around the Capitol complex can be a little confusing, but there are lots of security guards and staffers who are always happy to help you navigate it. The Capitol Building itself is actually divided into a House side and a Senate side, where each chamber meets. Across the street, there are three House Office Buildings: Cannon, Longworth, and Rayburn, which are connected by underground tunnels. On the other side of the Capitol, there are three Senate Office Buildings—Hart, Dirksen, and Russell—which are also connected by tunnels and a Senate subway. Every member of Congress has an office in one of these office buildings.

In Chapter 5 you advised that we should "be specific." So what specifically are we asking for during Museums Advocacy Day?

First of all, we're impressed that you've memorized the chapters—gold star for you! Each year, in cooperation with the Museums Advocacy Day Planning Committee, we determine the "asks," depending on a variety of political and policy considerations. The asks may be related to urging members of Congress to sign on to a letter to appropriators in support of increased funding for the IMLS Office of Museum Services, discuss the effect that the No Child Left Behind law has had on museums, or oppose amendments to reduce or eliminate funding for museums. We promise that after a full day of advocacy training, you'll be ready to advocate on all of these issues!

What is a "Dear Colleague" letter and why is it so important?

One of the primary ways that members of Congress communicate with each other is through "Dear Colleague" letters, which are letters that literally begin, "Dear Colleague." They can be on a variety of topics, including urging colleagues to co-sponsor a bill, sign on to a letter, take note of a news article, participate in an event, or otherwise ask a colleague to take some action or be part of an effort.

An excellent example of this is the annual Dear Colleague letter circulated on Capitol Hill asking members of Congress to sign on to a letter to appropriators requesting increased funding for the Institute of Museum and Library Services Office of Museum Services (OMS). Generally, Dear Colleague letters that garner 200-plus signatures have a far better chance of being acted on than those that receive, say, 50 or 60 signatures.

Where can I find useful statistics to help me make my case?

You can use the Advocacy Inventory in Chapter 3 to make the case for your individual museum. AAM also has valuable resources, including the Museum Financial Information survey, a museum factsheet available on AAM's advocacy website www.speakupformuseums.org, and ongoing research studies available on AAM's website www.aam-us.org. The *2009 Museum Financial Information* includes the latest national benchmarking data on a wide array of museum operations. The book is available through The AAM Press Bookstore on the AAM website. In 2011, AAM plans to launch a national online data gathering and museum benchmarking system that will update constantly. Watch the AAM website for announcements.

The Institute of Museum and Library Services (IMLS) also has many excellent resources and studies that can be found on www.imls.gov.

Several other national affiliate organizations also have conducted useful studies.

It should be noted that in order to have useful statistics to help us make our case, reliable data must exist. You can do your part by participating in research studies from IMLS, AAM and other museum service organizations.

Are you sometimes asked for the same information from more than one organization? Sure, and the museum field is working to consolidate its data collection efforts. But remember that you are helping the entire field create meaningful advocacy tools every time you share information about your own museum.

What about finding statistics on the state level?
The U.S. Travel Association has useful statistics on the economic impact of travel and tourism (by state) here: http://poweroftravel.org/statistics/.

Americans for the Arts has state-by-state information on the economic impact of the arts and culture here: http://www.artsusa.org/information_ services/research/services/economic_impact/default.asp.

Your state government's websites—the Department of Education, Depart-ment of Taxation, Department of Economic Development, or Department of Cultural Affairs, for example—may also have useful information.

You can also visit websites for your state or regional museum association, state historic preservation offices, state arts agencies, state humanities councils, tribal historic preservation offices, state nonprofit associations, and more.

I really prefer using the good, old-fashioned telephone or pen and paper. Can I still be an advocate?
Of course you can. You can always call the Capitol switchboard at 202-224-3121 to reach members of Congress. Or you can grab your phonebook and look up your local elected government officials at all levels. Then give them a call or write a good, old-fashioned letter. There is still a certain appeal to receiving a handwritten—and heartfelt—letter. In any case, if you are a constituent, they want to hear from you!

Keep in mind the most important way to communicate with your legislators is with a personalized message. Most correspondence from constituents is handled the same way, whether it arrives as an email, phone call, or handwritten letter. So the truth is that contact by any means is going to be effective, and given that the AAM advocacy website allows you to personalize your emails with details about your museum, it can be just as effective as that handwritten letter.

This is all really helpful, but I want to explore some more Congressional resources. Where should I look?

Start with THOMAS (www.thomas.gov), a public website run by the Library of Congress that has many resources to help you follow legislation, research issues, and learn about Congressional history and procedures.

The House website (www.house.gov) is a great place to learn more about the House of Representatives, its members, committees, hearings, schedules, visitor information, educational resources, and more.

Likewise, the Senate website (www.senate.gov) has information about members, hearings, committees, schedules, votes, history, rules, and procedures. The Senate site also includes a very helpful glossary of countless legislative and procedural terms in the "Reference" section.

Did you know there are three C-SPAN channels? If so, you will just love this: C-SPAN is also online, again with lots of audio and video feeds, programming, history, information about the Administration, the Courts, transcripts of various political events, and a searchable video archive. You can even catch a session of the British House of Commons Prime Minister's Questions. It's very entertaining!

What is the Congressional Record?

The Congressional Record is a daily compendium of all the proceedings in the U.S. Congress. It contains records of debates, votes, speeches, bills that are introduced and considered, and statements that are submitted by members of Congress.

Members of Congress are often willing to submit a statement for the record in celebration or recognition of individuals or institutions in their district or state, and may have a staff person assigned to handle these statements. Some examples of these statements for the record are a significant milestone or anniversary, a new project, heroism, community service, educational achievement, or another noteworthy accomplishment by an individual or institution.

In fact, many members of Congress will jump at the chance to submit a statement in the Congressional Record in recognition of a local museum, such as when it has been awarded accreditation (or re-accreditation), or if the museum is participating in the Museum Assessment Program (MAP), which AAM jointly administers through a cooperative agreement with the federal Institute of Museum and Library Services.

If your museum has been awarded accreditation or is participating in MAP, visit www.speakupformuseums.org to send a special letter to your members of Congress to let them know about this accomplishment.

The Congressional Record is also a good way to research your members of Congress and the issues they are focused on. You can search the Congressional Record here: http://www.gpoaccess.gov/crecord/ or search it by member of Congress here: http://thomas.loc.gov/.

How are federal regulations developed and what is the Federal Register?

Federal agencies are tasked with developing rules and regulations on a range of issues, often related to legislation after it has become law. Each day, the federal government publishes the Federal Register, which contains proposed regulations, final regulations, notices about public comment periods, funding priorities, grant application deadlines, notices about upcoming public meetings, and other agency activity. You can search the online Federal Register here: http://www.federalregister.gov/.

You can also take a more active role in how regulations are determined by visiting www.regulations.gov. On this site, you can search proposed regulations, submit a comment on regulations, search information by agency, and sign up for email alerts about a specific regulation.

How can I become more involved in advocating for the nonprofit sector?

Most museums are 501(c)(3) tax-exempt, nonprofit organizations, and are greatly affected by many laws that Congress passes, including charitable giving incentives, nonprofit governance, capacity building, and more. AAM is proud to work with several national organizations, including Independent Sector (www.independentsector.org) and the National Council of Nonprofits (www.councilofnonprofits.org) on these and other issues. AAM also has a more detailed Issue Brief and letter templates on its advocacy website, www. speakupformuseums.org, to help you learn more about these issues and get involved as an advocate.

Alphabet soup is tasty, but can you help me decipher these acronyms? And how can I contact federal agencies?

CBO = Congressional Budget Office – www.cbo.gov/

DHS = U.S. Department of Homeland Security – http://www.dhs.gov/

DOD = U.S. Department of Defense – www.defense.gov/

DOE = U.S. Department of Education – http://www.ed.gov/

DOI   = U.S. Department of Interior – http://www.doi.gov/

DOL = U.S. Department of Labor – www.dol.gov/

DOS = U.S. Department of State – http://www.state.gov/

EPA   = Environmental Protection Agency – http://epa.gov/

HHS = U.S. Department of Health and Human Services – http://www.hhs.gov/

IACB = Indian Arts and Crafts Board – www.iacb.doi.gov/

IMLS = Institute of Museum and Library Services – http://imls.gov/

IRS   = Internal Revenue Service – http://www.irs.gov/

LOC = Library of Congress – http://www.loc.gov/

NARA = National Archives and Records Administration – http://www.archives.gov/

National NAGPRA Office = Office within the National Park Service that administers the Native American Graves Protection and Repatriation Act – http://www.nps.gov/history/nagpra/

NEA = National Endowment for the Arts – http://www.nea.gov/

NEH = National Endowment for the Humanities – http://www.neh.gov/

NOAA = National Oceanic and Atmospheric Administration – http://www.noaa.gov/

NPS = National Park Service – http://www.nps.gov/index.htm

NSF = National Science Foundation – http://www.nsf.gov/

NTIA = National Telecommunications and Information Administration – http://www.ntia.doc.gov/

OMB = Office of Management and Budget – www.whitehouse.gov/omb/

USDA = U.S. Department of Agriculture – http://www.usda.gov

If you are looking for any other federal entity, visit: http://www.usa.gov/

How can I find out about federal grants?

Some members of Congress have a staff person assigned to help organizations identify appropriate grant opportunities, which means there is someone waiting for you to call and ask this question!

You can also visit: http://grants.gov/ or visit AAM's Information Center, which is also a resource.

These days, you can often go directly to the source by visiting federal agency websites (see above) and signing up for their email announcements.

What does a Congressional office look like?

In some ways, each Congressional office operates like a small business. There are different structures, staff assignments, rules, cultures, etc., from office to office.

A member of Congress usually has a Chief of Staff, who manages all of the member's offices. There is usually a State Director (in a Senate office) or a District Director (in a House office), who manages the state or local office(s).

A Legislative Director (or "LD") oversees all legislation, bills, votes, correspondence around issues, and may serve as the key staff person for a committee assignment.

A Communications Director or Press Secretary handles all media calls, arranges press events, writes press releases or media statements, and often does a lot of outreach with constituents through newsletters and social media. He or she is usually located in Washington, DC, but is sometimes located in a district or state office.

There are usually several Legislative Assistants (or "LAs") who are each assigned a portfolio of legislative issues (agriculture, education, foreign affairs, health care, or veterans, for example). The portfolio can be one or two issues or as many as a dozen or more, so these staffers are pulled in many directions on any given day. Senate offices typically have more Legislative Assistants who focus on a smaller portfolio of issues.

The Scheduler/Executive Assistant may have the toughest job, as he or she gets an overwhelming number of requests for the member of Congress's time and often has to squeeze too many things into a given day. They have the added challenge of having to contend with a constantly changing schedule due to circumstances beyond their control (hats off to them!). Senate offices may have more than one person serving in this role.

A Legislative Correspondent (or "LC") is assigned to respond to all constituent contact (mail, phone calls, petitions, etc.), or to coordinate this effort for the entire office. In the Senate, a Legislative Correspondent may assist a specific Legislative Assistant with his or her portfolio of issues and respond to constituents on those issues.

A Legislative Aide is often a hybrid of a Legislative Assistant and a Legislative Correspondent.

A Staff Assistant usually greets visitors, answers the phone, sorts mail, assists with letter writing, and manages interns, among other tasks. A Senate office will typically have several Staff Assistants.

The Systems Administrator oversees all technical and computer aspects of the office, including managing the constituent database, which might include you if you have had previous contact with the office or the office has obtained a publicly available voter file and you are a registered voter!

Caseworkers help constituents cut through red tape at federal agencies (Social Security, Veterans Affairs, Internal Revenue Service, etc.) and are usually based in the state or district office.

There are usually several Field Representatives (based in the state or district office) who are often assigned a portfolio of issues and they interact with the community on those issues. Their job is to be visible in the community—attending events, making public remarks, presenting certificates, and generally standing in for the member of Congress when he or she is not available. There is probably someone assigned to education issues: he or she would be a good person to get to know, especially since their job is to get to know you and your institution!

There may also be a Grants Coordinator whose job is to help community organizations (like your museum) identify potential grant opportunities.

All offices are likely to have interns, and my best advice about interns is to be extra nice to them. They are often very politically connected, ambitious, and may run for office someday. Some of my former interns have risen to serve as Chiefs of Staff and Legislative Directors on Capitol Hill. (I'm very proud!)

As noted above, Senate offices have more staff than House offices because they usually have more constituents to serve and represent (and consequently a larger budget). They may also have a Director of Special Projects and others who work on issues in a local community that affect a larger number of constituents. The size of the Washington, DC, office depends on the size of the state he or she represents.

Regardless of anyone's position or title, remember that everyone in these offices works for you: the taxpayer, the constituent, the advocate!

Do the congressional committees all have staff? How are they set up?

Each congressional committee also has a staff, some of whom work for the majority party, and fewer of whom work for the minority party.

There is a Staff Director, who serves as the top advisor to the Committee Chair on policy and strategy, and a Minority Staff Director, who serves similarly for the Ranking Minority Member of the Committee.

A committee will also have a Chief Counsel or General Counsel, who oversees all legislative, oversight, and investigative activities, and one or more Counsels who are assigned a specific portfolio of issues on which they will arrange hearings, draft legislation, organize mark-ups, and explore policy issues.

A nonpartisan Clerk handles all the records of the committee, including reports, votes, and legislation the committee takes up.

There are usually several Professional Staff Members, who are experts in specific policy areas, may have duties similar to those of Counsels, and who work with other members of Congress, federal agencies, and outside advocacy organizations.

There may also be Policy Directors who manage a subset of committee issues, and Policy Analysts who conduct research and work with Counsels or Professional Staff Members. Policy Advisors may have duties similar to Professional Staff Members.

There is also usually an Office Manager, a Staff Assistant, and Interns, all of whom are responsible for many important administrative functions of the committee.

Subcommittees may have a similar structure to the full committee, but fewer staff.

I know I learned this on Schoolhouse Rock when I was a kid, but how exactly does a bill become a law?

Since we can't sing "I'm Just a Bill" right here in this book (Darn. But you can find it on the Internet!), here's my version of how it works, step by step.

1. Have an Idea. Anyone can come up with an idea for a bill—the elected official, a member of the staff, the news media, or even a constituent. Some bills are complex; some are just a few sentences.

2. Draft the Bill. If a member of Congress wishes to introduce a bill, he or she will usually take the idea to the House or Senate Office of Legislative Counsel, an internal Congressional office where bill ideas are turned into "legislative language."

3. Gather Input. A member of Congress will often solicit input and support from constituents and other stakeholders.

4. Introduce It. Members of Congress can introduce as many bills as they wish. Once it is introduced, it receives a number (H.R. 10 or S. 298, for example).

5. Get to Committee. A bill is then referred to one or more committees (in the House) or one committee (in the Senate), and sometimes a series of subcommittees.

6. Hold a Hearing. A committee or subcommittee may choose to learn more about the bill by holding one or more hearings.

7. Hold a Markup. If a committee wants to take action, it will usually hold what's called a "mark up," where the bill could be "marked up" with amendments or other changes and then (hopefully) passed.

8. Write a Committee Report. If the committee passes the bill, the committee staff will usually prepare a written report about the bill, indicating pros and cons, administration views, intent and scope of the bill, etc.

9. Go to the Floor. The bill could then go to the House or Senate floor. The Senate gets right to work, debating the bill, offering amendments, and then voting on final passage. In the House, there is one additional step: the Rules

Committee will first decide how the bill will be considered (if amendments may be offered, etc.).

10. Or Have a Motion to Recommit. The bill could be referred back to a committee for specific changes to be made, thus delaying final passage.

11. Get Referred to the Other Chamber. If the bill passes the House, it goes to the Senate. If it passes the Senate, it goes to the House.

12. Get Taken Up Again! The other chamber (House or Senate) will next go through a process similar to the first chamber. The bill may be changed, approved, defeated, or simply ignored.

13. Reconcile any Differences. If the House and Senate each passes a different version of a bill, a Conference Committee is formed to iron out any differences. "Conferees" from both the House and Senate are appointed to serve on the committee.

14. Write Another Report. If the differences can be worked out, they file a Conference Report, which then has to pass each chamber once again.

15. Pass the House and Senate Again! Hopefully, the House and Senate pass the reconciled version of the bill.

16. Get Signed by the President. If both chambers approve the Conference report, the bill goes to the president to be signed into law. (After all that, is what you originally wanted still in there?)

17. Issue a Signing Statement. Sometimes the president will issue a statement about the legislation being signed into law. The statement may support the intent of the bill, emphasize the need for the bill, express concerns about the bill, or even question the constitutionality of the bill.

18. Or Get Vetoed. The president may sign the bill, or veto it, or even ignore it (called a "pocket veto").

19. And Possibly Get Overridden. If there is a presidential veto, the House and Senate may override the veto with a two-thirds vote in each chamber.

20. Get Regulations. Depending on the type of bill, a federal agency will usually be in charge of implementing or enforcing a particular law. The law may call for federal regulations to set forth how a bill will be implemented. Sometimes it is unclear how the law should be interpreted, either by a federal agency or by the courts. In these cases, agency officials will consider the legislative history of a bill, which includes all public records of statements, votes, and deliberations to determine Congressional intent. Or the bill ends up in court.

See, it's easy as pie.

Actually, there are so many places along the way where a bill can get blocked, tabled, or ignored altogether; it's a wonder anything ever makes it through. Perhaps this is the best argument yet for the importance of patience and persistence!

We hope you will let us know how you used this information, and pass along your other favorite resources so we can share them with other advocates.

"Before beginning a hunt, it is wise to ask someone what you are looking for before you begin looking for it."

– Winnie the Pooh,
from Pooh's Little Instruction Book, inspired by A.A. Milne

Chapter 10

Advice from the Field: What Works For Your Colleagues

Mary Ellen Pelzer, President and CEO, South Street Seaport Museum, New York City

"Get the people that you are involved with to help you: your board members, your super volunteers, your corporate sponsors. These people all know other people.

"Start locally. People on city council all know who is on our state assembly, and they know who is in Congress, and they all talk to each other.

"We've been holding Census training at the museum, and that's been enormously popular with everyone. We have a lot of free space at the museum and it was good for us to give back to the people we ask so much from frequently. That's one of the things that is important for a good advocate—to be a good listener to see what they need, and often what they need is for you to be a good organization, a professional organization, and to care about the community that you are in. A simple thing like giving space to the Census [Bureau] can be helpful. There are things like that in every community."

"Tell everybody that you are doing this. I let everybody know that I'm coming to Washington, that I'm in Washington, and that I've just gotten back. And this is very helpful. I tell people who I've visited with, why I talked to them, and inevitably what will happen is so-and-so who I deal with at the Department of Transportation will say, 'Oh, you just met with Congressman X's staff?' And he will send off an email, 'I don't know what they came and talked to you about, but I want you to know that I love the South Street Seaport Museum and the programs that they do.' That means a lot, building that network within your community. That's good fundraising, good advocacy with corporations, that affects other people. If you have a good reputation in your community, then that will be known.

"Work with your board. This is a wonderful opportunity for them to help you. For most of their businesses, they frequently deal with these same topics, and it's very easy for them to get started in helping you in this way."

Kathy Kelsey Foley, Director, Leigh Yawkey Woodson Art Museum, Wausau, Wisc.

"Say 'thank you' as often as possible, and mean it. Not only when you get something but just because…Don't take legislators or their staff for granted…Acknowledge their good work even if it is not related to our [museum] work.

"Build Relationships. People do things for people they know. Get to know your legislators—local, state, federal—as well as their staff members. It's important to develop these relationships at all levels because you don't know if the alderman has his or her sights on the state legislature, or if the senator has his or her sights on the governor's mansion, and so on. And it's not improbable that a staff person would one day run for office.

"Ask what you can do, how you can be helpful, how your institution can be helpful—meaning you're not always asking for something. Asking how you can be helpful is a natural outgrowth of developing relationships. Examples: consider opportunities to put your legislators in the spotlight—your institutional spotlight—which is a win-win, especially when you can get media coverage…One of our state legislators who is a champion of education had the opportunity to attend [an event] at the Woodson Art Museum during which elementary school children, her constituents, were in attendance, as well as their parents and chaperones, all likely voters. It was a great media opportunity, a great visual (as opposed to a grin and grab). Everybody wins.

"Keep legislators and elected officials and their staffs informed, up to date, and in the know. This includes press releases, invitations, general mailings. Also be conscious of sharing time-sensitive breaking news if it's appropriate or possible…It's better that legislators on the state, local, or federal level don't read your important news in the newspaper…You want to be the one who provided the heads-up. An example might be the launch of a major building project, an expansion, or a major bequest, especially if it came from a constituent. Even a major acquisition would be something to share under the heading of a heads-up.

"You could become a fan [of legislators] on Facebook, or invite them to be a fan of your museum's Facebook page.

"Say 'thank you' again. Remember to say 'please,' too. Those courtesies go a long way. Handwritten notes are still meaningful, perhaps even more so today, especially in this age of digital communication."

Brenda Raney, Director of Government Relations, Science Museum of Minnesota, St. Paul, Minn.

"Keep your ear to the ground, keep up on new committee assignments, new staff members. Simple things, personal things, like their child is growing up and going to college. Where are they going to go? Knowing that kind of info helps you build that relationship.

"Always be informing them about what's going on at your museum. Keep your museum on their mind. Send press releases to their district offices or to their state offices…If you can get them on your membership list, that would be fantastic. If you do a newsletter, send that out. Make sure that it's sitting on the coffee table of the district office. Where it's appropriate, draw a connection for the legislator between their initiatives and the work you are doing at your museum…If you say, 'See this program that we are doing on Saturday mornings for kids, this is in direct connection to the work you are doing trying to pass the No Child Left Inside Act,' or something like that.

"Make sure you invite legislators to things at your museum, and this goes beyond opening events…Think about what it is that your legislators do. We have a legislator who is on a committee that helps us at the state level and he is a former teacher. So when his school—the district that he used to teach in—was coming to our museum for some professional development activities that we sponsor, we made sure to invite him. He came. He talked to constituents. He loved it because it made him feel like a teacher again and it made a great impression, and he's been a good friend ever since. So think about things like that. Again, going back to your research, knowing your legislators, and finding opportunities to get them at your museum interacting with the things that you do best. And if you can throw in a few real people and a few real staff for them to talk to, even better.

"Collaborate with other people in your community, and I would challenge you to think creatively about who those people are.

"Some are the folks that we collaborate with at the Science Museum of Minnesota include the Minnesota High Tech Association, the Chamber of Commerce, the Minnesota Business Partnership, organizations that you might not necessarily think really tie well with museums. But we all have a common goal of increasing workforce development, increasing STEM [Science, Technology, Engineering and Mathematics] education in the state of Minnesota. Things like that are universal among all of us, and by partnering and collaborating with those folks, our message is at the table when they're talking to people, and it brings up our level of awareness among a group that might ordinarily be out of the caucus that we normally deal with. It's actually paid us great dividends in the past and I think will continue to do so in the future."

Jeff Hamilton, Director of Governmental and Community Relations, Exploratorium, San Francisco, Calif.

"You can think of your museum as a stage on which you get to conduct this [advocacy] process. Unlike a lot of people lobbying government—and I can say this having been lobbied—what you've got is really interesting. It's fun to go to a museum. It's fun to play at the Exploratorium. And every political leader and public official I've engaged with so far has a deep visceral and emotional connection with their memories of a museum. So that's where you want to go.

"And then of course, your accomplishments, your statistics, your impact. For example, we train 400 science teachers a year. We have 300,000 children visit the museum a year. We have all those sorts of statistics at hand.

"Start with your board. I keep a list of my board with me all the time because when I get stumped and I think, 'How are we going to get at this issue?' I can immediately look at that list.

"Trust in and cultivate your passion for your institution. Politicians and public officials don't need another slick operator. You just need to be happy and enthusiastic about your institution. You really do have—we have—what people want, which is to be inspired, turned on, to be excited, to learn. You can't bottle that. We have this magical thing that everyone wants to be part of. So use that in whatever imaginative, fun, crazy way you can think of to advance your relationship with whatever level of government you engage with."

Jenny Benjamin, Director, and sole staff member, of the Museum of Vision, San Francisco, Calif.

"As the only employee at my institution, there's a lot to do. I have to balance exhibits, curatorial duty, collections, so it's not easy. But I did make the choice to add Advocacy to my workload. Initially, I did that to represent members of [AAM's] Small Museums Administrators Committee. I am the chair and I felt it was my duty to make sure that federal funding is available to all small museums. Increased funding for IMLS would hopefully trigger [federal-state partnership] grants, which would be a big boon to small museums. I also had a little insight. I have two sisters, and they worked for congresspeople during their early careers. They were very insistent that I go because they knew that every voice that goes to Congress, every letter you write, is incredibly important. And that congresspeople really sit up and listen when people take the trouble to actually talk to them, instead of complaining. So with that incentive, I did go to Washington, DC. Also, AAM made it exceptionally easy, which was very important to me. I knew they were going to train me, I knew they were going to set all my appointments so I didn't have to worry. Obviously, talking to members of Congress can be a little nerve-wracking, but it was a great experience. The most interesting part of my day was over lunch ... I assumed that the cafeteria would be filled with staff people and maybe some tourists. But the people I was eating lunch with down there were all lobbyists. They were all people like me, actually, and I didn't meet anyone who was doing something I really hated. I met people from the teachers association, I met open space advocates, and I loved them all. I loved their causes, and I thought, 'We should have been here before now, because if I like their causes, I bet their congresspeople do, too!' So I thought: 'My goodness, we're Johnny-come-lately, and I just found this in the cafeteria for the first time!'

"Now, being from a small museum, I spend a lot of time scheduling my year, and I expected that Advocacy Day would be just that, one day, and I would come home and maybe next year I would think about going again... While in DC, a colleague of mine, Elsa Bailey, was asked by our local congresswoman to make a presentation to her district office and a local council that she had set up, and I was sort of taken aback. This meant I had to take Advocacy Day home. We put together a group of other small museums, a group of museums, by the way, that I never met, had no previous contact with. I called them out of the blue. I said, 'Your congresswoman wants to know about you,' and everybody came. Everybody came because they realized that here was a way for everyone who didn't get to go to DC to still do that. The district office was very nice, the local council was made up of local elected officials, business leaders, union leaders, people I hadn't had a lot of contact with before. They asked good questions and they were interested in us and suddenly Advocacy Day not only led to federal advocacy but also local advocacy came into the picture...The local paper came to cover it so we all got in the paper, too. This was a huge benefit...Advocacy raised the profile of about a dozen small museums in our district and so now I'm planning on keeping advocacy in my day-to-day schedule because of this great experience, and I hope my words will help you to feel the same way."

Leslie Findlen, vice president of development, Brooklyn Botanic Garden, Brooklyn, NY

"I've worked in development for so many years. But I'm always asking for someone else's dollars. And I realized that was something I had missed in thinking about elected officials internally, because I was thinking I was asking for *their* dollars, and being in Washington, DC, reminded me that I was asking for *my* dollars. I'm asking for *our* dollars. When I look at my paycheck, I see how much is [being taken out]. It's a lot. And that makes me stop and think, 'How do I want that to be used to shape my community?' I work at a museum because I believe certain things and I believe [museums] are powerful aspects to shaping healthy communities. So in climates like this—and I really believe crisis is an opportunity—it engages and focuses people. It really gave me a much more empowered sense of talking to elected officials. Of course I will always be respectful and polite, but I will never forget ultimately that I'm advocating and asking for the use of my community's dollars—or my dollars, on a more personal level."

Karen Witter, Associate Director of the Illinois State Museum, Springfield, Ill., and former member of the Illinois governor's staff.

"Part of my job was to work with a multitude of interest groups. I was a policy advisor on environmental issues and dealt with everything from agriculture to nuclear safety to environmental protection. That involved determining what constituencies had to say, and it was a cacophony of things. We dealt with interest groups day in and day out, and we wrote bill reviews for the governor. What should his position be on this piece of legislation? We wanted to have all of those voices represented to the governor on what he should do. I have to say, at that point in time, I have no recollection of an organized museum constituency expressing its voice on any of those issues.

"I was dealing with natural resources issues, but my colleagues were dealing with all kinds of other issues, and with the possible exception of Museums in the Park that spoke for and advocated for the largest museums in Chicago, I simply have no recollection of a museum voice at all in that arena.

"The most effective organizations had behind them a network of people throughout the state. In many cases it was a very strong grassroots movement. You knew the person speaking to you represented a broad constituency base. For example, the soil and water conservation districts were notorious because anytime their [funding] was threatened, they churned out letters from every single county in the state. The reaction was that it's not worth messing with the soil and water conservation districts because they are so active in their opposition to any kind of cut and they could mobilize an aggressive, organized grassroots effort.

"Recently the Illinois Arts Council was threatened with very significant budget cuts in the state. The response from the Illinois Arts Alliance, which is the advocacy coalition for the arts council, was instantaneous. They emailed their members with easy ways to find your legislators and respond with a consistent message. They also had a media campaign about what the impact would be. They had studied the national situation…They had done a survey, they had all of the statistics, and they were very well organized.

"In contrast, the Illinois Association of Museums had received state support for staff for the last ten years or so. That funding was proposed to be taken away. There was a lot of concern. There was a lot of, "Oh, my gosh," but there was no organized, instantaneous response to that. The infrastructure for an organized response was simply not in place.

"Something I want to talk about is the difference between field-wide advocacy and making sure national spokespeople know that they are backed up by a large number of constituents, and then individual advocacy and what you need to do to participate at both levels. I really want to commend AAM for bringing forward Museums Advocacy Day, but their power comes from speaking with a united voice across the whole constituency. And that's all of us. If we don't implement a field-wide effort, AAM cannot be an effective advocate on behalf of all of us. So when they are speaking in Washington, we have to take that message back home, in terms of our individual Congressional districts.

"There are simple ways to participate. Do little things, but do them often. Ask a teacher or a student who was impacted by your program to write to the elected official. Get quotes from those people and pass them on to the people in your organization who are more responsible for advocacy. But don't let people use the 'that's their job' excuse. I work within a state agency and there are certain things I can't do, so partially you want to fly below the radar. But if you ask a teacher to send a letter to an elected official, [that should be okay.]

"Get to know the staffs of your elected officials. The importance of staff is just monumental. You might have the opportunity for what we call the 'grip and grin' photograph, and have your photograph taken with a legislator, and that's all wonderful. But the staff person is the one who is writing the policy brief, who is talking to the constituents, who is getting impassioned, and who is knowing closer to the ground what is going on. They are the ones who are going to decide whether that member of Congress is going to attend an event, or put your phone call through, or make those kinds of contacts.

"They are gatekeepers, policy advisors, conduits to access, and they influence the schedule. They can be very important, so never [...] think you are 'only' meeting with staff.

"Look for creative opportunities to partner. We happen to be next to the state capitol. We had an African American sculpture exhibit, and we really wanted our Legislative Black Caucus to see it. We didn't know if they would come. But lo and behold, they needed to have a reception for one of their key members who was retiring from the General Assembly. We said we'd be glad to be the venue. We could do that because we weren't lobbying for a specific cause, but we were just a venue for an event."

Congratulations! Today is your day.
You're off to Great Places! You're off and away!...
And will you succeed? Yes! You will, indeed!
(98 and 3/4 percent guaranteed.)

– Oh, the Places You'll Go by Dr. Seuss

Chapter 11

And Now: Advocating for Me

Okay, now you know all about advocating for museums. And hopefully, you are excited to get started.

But first, let's take a moment to consider how AAM can help you become a great advocate—for *yourself!*

So how can AAM help you advance your own career?

We're glad you asked! There are lots of ways that AAM can help, starting when you join as a member of the American Association of Museums. Not only are AAM's advocacy efforts more powerful when they are backed by robust membership numbers, but AAM membership also provides you with discounted access to numerous opportunities for professional development and networking, job leads, books, and much more. Here is a summary:

1. Take full advantage of AAM's professional development offerings: live and on-demand webinars, face-to-face seminars and workshops, AAM podcasts, online learning communities, and more at www.aam-us.org. Encourage your institution to join AAM so you can access the full menu of programs at a discount.

2. Visit JobHQ at www.aam-us.org. AAM's online job headquarters lists museum jobs across the country and is free for those applying.

3. Align with Field-Wide Standards and Ethics. The AAM standards—known as the *Characteristics of Excellence for U.S. Museums*—and the ethical guidelines, *Code of Ethics for U.S. Museums*—are critical tools to help you advocate for your museum and communicate its value to society. These documents help policymakers, the media, philanthropic organizations, donors and members of the public assess your museum's achievements and operations. AAM Accreditation is a highly regarded seal of approval that brings national recognition to a museum for its commitment to excellence, accountability, high professional standards, and continued institutional improvement. The Museum Assessment Program (MAP) is a terrific way to advance your own skills while assessing and building capacity within your museum.

4. Join a professional network. AAM offers you the opportunity to join one or more of its Standing Professional Committees or Professional Interest Committees, designed to help you connect with others who work in your area of expertise or share common interests. Find out more on AAM's website.

5. Visit AAM's Information Center. There you can develop your skills on grant writing, donor development, accountability, collections issues, community engagement, and much more. Also reachable via www.aam-us.org.

6. Get Steep Discounts at The AAM Press Bookstore. You've already gotten a great start by reading this book (thanks!). Now check out other titles available. You can get the latest on best practices in your current field, or learn about the challenges and rewards of working in any area of museum operations. Check out our titles on accessibility, audience, collections stewardship, development, education, exhibits, facilities, governance, human resources, legal issues, marketing, public relations, sustainability, technology, volunteers, and much more.

7. See the Future! AAM's Center for the Future of Museums helps museums explore the cultural, political and economic challenges facing society and devise strategies to shape a better tomorrow. CFM is a think-tank and research and design lab for fostering creativity and helping museums transcend traditional boundaries to serve society in new ways.

8. Get Your Own Copy of *Museum* Magazine. Read and enjoy AAM's award-winning bimonthly magazine and stay current with all that's happening in the museum world, here in the U.S. and abroad.

9. Attend AAM's Annual Meeting and MuseumExpo™. As the largest gathering of museum professionals in the world, this is your premier networking and professional development opportunity. It's also a time to stop and think about your goals, your work, and get inspired. Plus, it's a lot of fun! You can get even more involved by submitting a session proposal or volunteering. Visit www.aam-us.org to learn more. We look forward to seeing you there!

This is only a sampling of AAM's current offerings. There is much more going on at AAM, so we invite you to join us and get involved.

We also recognize that we have much to learn from you and your colleagues in the field. We invite you to contact us with your questions, suggestions, and ideas so we can work together to support and advance museums—of all types, of all sizes, and from all regions—in all that we do.

It's up to all of us. Join us in the task!

Index